Galway Kinnell

Twayne's United States Authors Series

Frank Day, Editor

Clemson University

TUSAS 603

Galway Kinnell
Photograph by Caroline Croft

Galway Kinnell

Richard J. Calhoun

Clemson University

Twayne Publishers • New York
Maxwell Macmillan Canada • Toronto
Maxwell Macmillan International • New York Oxford Singapore Sydney

Galway Kinnell
Richard J. Calhoun

Macmillan Publishing Company

Twayne Publishers
Macmillan Publishing Company
866 Third Avenue
New York, New York 10022

Maxwell Macmillan Canada, Inc.
1200 Eglinton Avenue East
Suite 200
Don Mills, Ontario M3C 3N1

Macmillan Publishing Company is part of the Maxwell Communication Group of Companies.

10 9 8 7 6 5 4 3 2 1

The paper used in this publication meets the minimum requirements of American National Standard for Information Sciences—Permanence of Paper for Printed Library Materials. ANSI Z39.48-1984.

Printed and bound in the United States of America

Library of Congress Cataloging-in-Publication Data

Calhoun, Richard James.
Galway Kinnell / Richard J. Calhoun.
p. cm. — (Twayne's United States authors series ; TUSAS 603)
Includes bibliographical references and index.
ISBN 0-8057-3955-6
1. Kinnell, Galway, 1927- —Criticism and interpretation.
I. Title. II. Series.
PS3521.I582Z63 1992
811′.54—dc20 92-5023

To my wife, Doris, and to all my children—
Carolyn, Martin, and Becky; and a notation to the poet
whose poetry and criticism led me to an interest in
Galway Kinnell–James Dickey.

Contents

Preface

Galway Kinnell is one of our most accomplished poets, a fact that is one of the best kept secrets among contemporary writers, known only to a select group of poets who recognize his skills, a few critics who have consistently sung his praises, a loyal audience of readers who have appreciated the power of his poems, and almost everyone who has experienced the compelling readings that Kinnell gives to his poetry. Whether he is taught or not depends on the literary anthology used: in most, his poetry has small representation; in a few, an appropriately generous selection; in others, no representation at all. In literary histories, as far as current literary movements are concerned, Kinnell is neither a leader of a movement nor a follower. In the usual discussions of establishment and antiestablishment he has the distinction of not being recognizable as unmistakably either.

My own interest in Kinnell's poetry probably follows from my earlier interest in the poetry of James Dickey, with whom he has more than occasionally been mentioned in the same breath. He is sometimes compared and contrasted with his former Princeton contemporary and friend, W. S. Merwin. Kinnell could be better approached, as I am sure he would prefer, relative to either of two great predecessors with whom he has some lineage, Walt Whitman or Rainer Maria Rilke.

Galway Kinnell's literary output is abundant and varied. He has written major volumes of poetry and a novel, compiled four volumes of translations and a collection of essays and interviews, and drawn illustrations for a children's book. Recently, with poetry residency at New York University, he has become what has always transmitted a sense of status, a *New Yorker* magazine regular as a poet. At long last he is receiving book-length critical notice, with the recent publication of a collection of critical essays and a full-dress critical analysis of his poetry. Both studies are recognized in this text as part of the significant recent critical interest in him as a poet. Kinnell is not quite a man of letters, as versatile in more than one literary form as were Allen Tate or Randall Jarrell, or as James Dickey is. His primary mission is poetry, but I have attempted to stress the quality and the relevance of his criticism, though it is not large in quantity. I do not attempt much of a case for Galway Kinnell as a novelist; such an assessment would be premature, for it would be based on only one novel. A strong argument should be made, but not here, for Galway Kinnell as a major translator of French literature, with special accolades given for his translations of François Villon. Several of these poems in English are quite remarkable.

Galway Kinnell's preoccupations as a poet are easy to identify. It is harder to designate much development in poetic themes, but it is subtly there. I strongly contend that Kinnell has too often been viewed as undeviatingly concerned with our engagement with all other living things in the process of dying and death. He is perceived as gloomily intent on finding some means of understanding for the common mortality of all living things. Some critics have blindly tried to imply a consistent style for redundant themes. I have tried to demonstrate that both views—of his themes and of his style—are at the least too facile, and at the most downright wrong.

My approach proposes that Galway Kinnell's achievements as a poet are best seen as part of an evolution on his part, shared, in different ways, with poets of his generation, from the modernism of Eliot and Pound to his own use of the postmodernist explorations into the personal of poets like Theodore Roethke and Robert Lowell. Kinnell quickly became an important, if still unacknowledged, postmodernist—personal but still universal, more direct than ambiguously indirect, more narrative than symbolist, characteristically more surrealistic than realistic, and freer in verse and looser in structure than he had been while attempting, in his earliest verse, to write the well-made poem according to the strictures of the New Criticism. In his most recent poetry Kinnell has even relaxed from his attempts at the long poem, written with primal intensity, to compose quieter and simpler poems about more ordinary things. I stress that these are noteworthy poems. I put considerable emphasis on what Kinnell as a poet—who began writing in the immediate post–World War II phase of admiration for Yeats, Eliot, and Auden as the exemplars and the New Criticism as the doctrine—became in the altered poetic climate of the sixties, seventies, and eighties.

I wish to acknowledge the critical work of those who have written before me on Galway Kinnell, especially the astute criticism of Howard Nelson, Lee Zimmerman, Charles G. Bell, Richard Howard, Charles Molesworth, and Ralph J. Mills, all of whom have been substantially appreciative of the literary importance of Galway Kinnell. I owe something to the patience of Liz Traynor Fowler as this book, under the pressure of other commitments, suffered various delays. Above all, I owe much to the editorial skills and critical comments of my editor and friend, Frank Day.

Acknowledgments

Grateful acknowledgment is made to Houghton Mifflin for permission to reprint selections from the following volumes of Galway Kinnell's poetry:

What a Kingdom It Was, © 1960 by Galway Kinnell.

The Avenue Bearing the Initial of Christ into the New World, © 1953, 1954, © 1955, 1958, 1959, 1960, 1961, 1963, 1964, 1970, 1971, 1974 by Galway Kinnell.

Body Rags, © 1967 by Galway Kinnell.

Flower Herding on Mount Monadnock, © 1964 by Galway Kinnell.

The Book of Nightmares, © 1971 by Galway Kinnell.

Mortal Acts, Mortal Words, © 1980 by Galway Kinnell.

The Past, © 1985 by Galway Kinnell.

Acknowledgment is made to Alfred A. Knopf and Random House for permission to reprint selections from *When One Has Lived a Long Time Alone*, © 1990 by Galway Kinnell.

Acknowledgment is made to Galway Kinnell for permission to reprint selections from *Walking Down the Stairs: Selections from Interviews*, © 1978 by Galway Kinnell.

Ohio Review and Galway Kinnell for permission to quote from "An Interview with Wayne Dodd and Stanley Plumly," *Ohio Review* 14 (Fall 1972); © Galway Kinnell 1972.

Galway Kinnell for permission to quote from "Poetry, Personality, and Death," *Field*, no. 4 (Spring 1971); © 1971 by Galway Kinnell.

Galway Kinnell for permission to quote from "The Poetics of the Physical World," *Iowa Review* 2 (Summer 1971); © 1971 by Galway Kinnell.

Galway Kinnell for permission to publish from "Being with Reality: An Interview with Galway Kinnell," *Columbia: A Magazine of Poetry and Prose*, no. 14, 1989; © Galway Kinnell 1989.

Abbreviations

Citations from Galway Kinnell's works are identified by the following abbreviations:

BL	*Black Light.* Boston: Houghton Mifflin, 1965. The novel was reissued in 1980 by North Point Press, San Francisco.
BN	*The Book of Nightmares.* Boston: Houghton Mifflin, 1971.
BWR	"Being with Reality: An Interview with Galway Kinnell," *Columbia: A Magazine of Poetry and Prose,* no. 14 (1989): 169–82.
BR	*Body Rags.* Boston: Houghton Mifflin, 1968.
FH	*Flower Herding on Mount Monadnock.* Boston: Houghton Mifflin, 1964.
FP	*First Poems. The Avenue Bearing the Initial of Christ into the New World: Poems 1946–64.* Boston: Houghton Mifflin, 1974.
WOHLLTA	*When One Has Lived a Long Time Alone.* New York, Alfred A. Knopf, 1990.
MAMW	*Mortal Acts, Mortal Words.* Boston: Houghton Mifflin, 1980.
PPD	"Poetry, Personality and Death." *Field,* no. 4 (1971): 56–75. Reprinted in *A Field Guide to Poetry and Poetics,* Stuart Fiebert and David Young, eds. New York: Longman, 1980, 203–23.
PPW	"The Poetics of the Physical World." *Iowa Review* 2 (1971): 113–26.
TP	*The Past.* Boston: Houghton Mifflin, 1985.
WDS	*Walking Down the Stairs: Selections from Interviews.* Ann Arbor: The University of Michigan Press, 1978.
WKW	*What a Kingdom It Was.* Boston: Houghton Mifflin, 1960.

Chronology

1927	Galway Kinnell born 1 February in Providence, Rhode Island. Last of four children of immigrant parents, Elizabeth Mills, from Ireland, and James Scott Kinnell, a native of Scotland.
1932–1943	Attends public schools in Pawtucket, Rhode Island, until he receives a scholarship to Wilbraham Academy in Massachusetts for his senior year.
1944	Enrolls at Princeton University; meets fellow student and aspiring poet W. S. Merwin.
1944–1946	Military service in the U. S. Navy. Returns to Princeton for training in the naval officer training program.
1947	Follows Charles G. Bell, his teacher and mentor at Princeton, to Black Mountain College in North Carolina for early exposure to the "open form" theories of Charles Olson.
1948	Graduates from Princeton, *summa cum laude.*
1948–1949	Graduate work in English at the University of Rochester. Receives M. A.
1951–1955	Lives in Chicago. Works for the University of Chicago in its downtown educational program.
1955–1957	Studies in France on a Fulbright grant.
1957	Brother, Derry, killed in an automobile wreck.
1957–1959	Lives on the Lower East Side in New York City.
1959	Travels in Far East.
1959–1960	Fulbright lectureship in Iran.
1960	Publication of *What a Kingdom It Was.*
1961	Buys an abandoned farm in northern Vermont, near Sheffield, and moves there.

1963 Active in Civil Rights movement. Volunteer worker for voter registration campaign in Louisiana for the Congress of Racial Equality. Sentenced to a week in jail for his activities.

1964 *Flower Herding on Mount Monadnock* published.

1965 Marries Inés Delgado de Torres. Becomes involved in public readings against the war in Vietnam, including a well-publicized "Poets for Peace" reading at Town Hall in New York City. First edition of his *Poems of François Villon* published.

1966 Daughter, Maud, born. Novel, *Black Light,* published.

1968 Son, Finn Fergus, born. *Body Rags* published.

1969 Resides in Spain.

1970 Publishes volume of early work, *First Poems.*

1971 *The Book of Nightmares* is published.

1974 First volume of collected poems published, including his first three books, excluding *The Book of Nightmares.* Awarded Shelley Prize by the Poetry Society of America.

1975 Organizes a reading of Christopher Smart's *Jubilate Agno* by several poets. Receives the National Institute of Arts and Letters' Medal of Merit.

1978 Fulbright lectureship at the University of Nice, France. Second and revised edition of *Poems of François Villon* published.

1979 Visiting writer at MacQuarrie University, Sydney, Australia.

1979–1981 Lives in Honolulu, Hawaii.

1980 *Mortal Acts, Mortal Words* published.

1982 Organizer of antinuclear reading at Town Hall, New York City, by Poets Against the End of the World.

1983 Co-winner of the American Book Award; receives Pulitzer Prize for poetry for *Selected Poems.*

1983–1984 President of P. E. N., international writers organization.

1984 Awarded MacArthur Foundation Grant for creative work.

1985 *The Past* published. Divorce from Inés Delgado de Torres Kinnell. Appointed Samuel F. B. Morse Professor of Fine Arts at New York University.

1986 Wrote the introduction to *Selected Poetry of Hayden Carruth*.

1987 Edited *The Essential Whitman* for Essential Poets Series.

1988 Contributes with other poets to limited edition book, *Apparitions,* edited by John Ashbery.

1990 *When One Has Lived a Long Time Alone* published.

Chapter One
A Poet's Life and Backgrounds

A Poet Appears

Charles G. Bell, teaching poetry at Princeton University during the winter of 1946–47, was approached by "a dark-shocked student, looking more like a prizefighter than a literary man," who showed him a poem "maybe his first," a Wordsworthian sonnet with "no modern flair."[1] Nevertheless he was astounded by the "romantic fierceness" of the last couplet. This poem was written by a young man who, he recognized, "could go beyond any poetic limits assigned." The student poet was Galway Kinnell. What the older poet, who became Kinnell's mentor both at Princeton and in special courses at the celebrated Charles Olson–inspired Black Mountain School in the North Carolina mountains, surmised about the student became true of Kinnell as a mature poet. He does have the ability to go beyond any poetic limits ordinarily assigned to poets of his generation. By late fall of 1946 Kinnell had written for his teacher a four-page poem, "A Mourning Wake Among the Dead," later titled "Among the Tombs." Bell concludes: "The death-haunted, tragic Kinnell had already spoken, though it would take years for the fact to be recognized" (Bell, 25).

It has literally taken years, even decades, for Galway Kinnell to be perceived as the major poet that he is. Distinguished critics have praised him, not always without qualifications; reviewers have favorably reviewed his books, not without reservations about his unrelenting preoccupation with mortality; and, after a long wait in the wings, he has finally emerged on stage to win both the Pulitzer Prize and the American Book Award in the same year, 1983. Nevertheless, Galway Kinnell is still not as well-known publicly as James Dickey, or assigned as high a place among modern poets by critics as John Ashbery or James Merrill. The newest history of American literature, the *Columbia Literary History of the United States,* casts Kinnell as one of the "deep image poets" or "surrealist" poets (W. S. Merwin, Louis Simpson, and James Wright); those influenced by

Robert Bly as poet, editor, and theoretician in their efforts to find an alternative to modernism in poetry through recovering "deep image" material from the subconscious.[2] Kinnell's own glimpse into the unconscious as a "deep image" poet is distinct from Bly's and Wright's, but his characteristics as a poet are not sharply distinguished from Merwin's explorations of the unconscious depths except for recognition of Kinnell's obviously greater passion. A comparison between these two poets is apt because of their early acquaintance and their brotherhood in poetry as fellow students at Princeton.

James Dickey once opined that Kinnell was an imitation of Dickey, but this was simply a rather frivolous acknowledgment of another poet's similar concerns with the primitive "other" that has troubled Dickey in his own poetry.[3] Dickey early recognized their similarities and their differences, and he actually welcomed the slightly younger poet's first book of poetry as an authentic beginning by a poet who "recognized the difference between knowing something because you have been told it is so" and "knowing it because you have lived it" (Dickey, 135). Coming from James Dickey this was considerable praise; for Dickey poetry should never seem to come from books, from "garden variety" academic reading. The deeper the poet dug down into living, the better; the more terrifying the "other" in nature to humankind the more powerful the poetry. Kinnell's poetry must have given him both a shock of recognition and perhaps an anxiety from the likeness he perceived. But there is an ostensible difference between the two poets. What is compelling in Kinnell's poetry is not the power of the "other," as in Dickey's poetry, but rather a vivid sense of the physical actuality of a world where all living creatures are doomed to a physical dissolution, and Kinnell's acceptance, if not quite celebration, of a consequent shared mortality with all living things.

Biography So Far

Galway Kinnell was born on 1 February 1927, in Providence, Rhode Island. He was the last of four children of James Cott and Elizabeth Mills Kinnell, both of whom were immigrants to the United States; his father emigrating from Scotland; his mother from Ireland. Galway's father earned a living as a carpenter and as a part-time teacher of woodworking.

The family moved in 1932, during the great American depression, to Pawtucket, Rhode Island, where Galway attended public schools until he was awarded for his senior year a scholarship to the private Wilbraham Academy in Massachusetts. At the academy an English teacher, Roger Nye Lincoln, gave him his first encouragement to try his hand at creative writing. Kinnell's scholastic achievements at Wilbraham elevated his academic ambitions to the Ivy League. He entered Princeton University in 1944 during World War II, and it was there that he met W. S. Merwin. Their acquaintance was mutually beneficial; they read and frequently discussed poetry together. But Kinnell soon left academics for what turned out to be a circuitous wartime service in the U. S. Navy, returning to Princeton for the navy officer training program.

After military service Galway Kinnell spent the summer of 1947 at Black Mountain College because his friend and mentor Charles Bell taught there, but Kinnell has never been regarded as one of the Black Mountain school of poets. At Princeton he was a brilliant student, graduating *summa cum laude* in 1948. He went on to the University of Rochester for graduate work in English, receiving his M. A. there in 1949. From 1951–55 he lived in Chicago, working as supervisor of the liberal arts program at the University of Chicago's downtown campus. His literary interests were revived in 1955, when he received a Fulbright grant to France, where he lived for two years, teaching at the University of Grenoble and, at the same time, translating Rene Hardy's novel *Bitter Victory* into French. It was the moment of existentialism in French philosophy and the time of a small renaissance in French literature that significantly influenced the decade's literature.

Tragedy struck Kinnell's family in 1957, with the death of his brother, Derry, in an automobile accident, a catastrophe that he has movingly tried to come to terms with in several of his poems on death. During 1957–59 Kinnell lived on the Lower East Side in New York City. He then began an ambulatory career as poet-in-residence, first at Juniata College in Huntingdon, Pennsylvania; then at Colorado State University; at Reed College in Portland, Oregon; at the University of California at Irvine; and at the University of Iowa in its acclaimed writing program. His second Fulbright lectureship was during 1959–60 in then friendly Iran. Wherever Kinnell lived, he absorbed some portion of the culture of the place. Many details from his only novel so far, *Black Light,* were drawn from this experience. As a poet, he was not discovered in any of the younger poets series published during the fifties. He had spent so much time teaching and traveling, and he was so reluctant to publish his early apprenticeship verse, that his first book, *What a Kingdom It Was,* was not published until 1960, when he was 33 years old. He also excluded these earliest poems from the first selection of his verse a decade later in 1970.

In 1961 Kinnell moved back to the Northeast, buying an abandoned farm in northern Vermont. During 1963, with the outbreak of civil rights protests in the South, he became a social activist, working in the registration campaign for the Congress of Racial Equality in Louisiana. His activities resulted in a week in jail and eventually to the publication of one of the finer pieces of social criticism from that time, a poem about these political experiences, "The Last River." His second book of poetry, *Flower Herding on Mount Monadnock,* was published in 1964. In 1965 Kinnell married Inés Delgado de Torres, from whom he was divorced 20 years later. The couple had two children, Maud Natasha, born in 1966, and Finn Fergus, called Sancho in later poems, born in 1968. Both children became important subjects of a poetry that needed concerns beyond those of Kinnell's individual consciousness. During the war in Vietnam Kinnell was again politically engaged as an antiwar activist poet. In 1965 he participated in a significant protest by antiwar writers, the "Poets for Peace" reading at Town Hall, New York City. He joined in numerous additional readings in protest of the war. The movement produced little significant poetry, and Kinnell, except for one or two of his poems, which are arguably among the best poems contributed to the antiwar effort, did not add a decisive number of distinguished poems to the movement.

Galway Kinnell has certainly been a gifted translator of poetry. His facility in French has earned him a reputation as an excellent translator, certainly better than Robert Lowell, if not quite as sensitive to the dramatic potentials of the language as Richard Wilbur. In 1965 he published his splendid translation of *Poems of François Villon,* which was fashioned even better in its 1977 revision. His third book of poetry, *Body Rags,* and a translation of Yves Bonnefoy's *On the Motion and Immobility of Douve,* an influence on his own poetry, were published in 1968.

Kinnell moved overseas again in 1968, living in Spain during 1969 with his Spanish wife, Inés, an episode that did not influence his poetry as decisively as his time spent in France. In 1970 he published a selection from his early poetry, but not from the earliest, under the title *First Poems* as well as a translation of Yvan Goll's *Lackawanna Elegy.* In 1971 *The Book of Nightmares,* arguably his most distinguished volume of poetry to date, was published. Three years later, in 1974, he made his first attempt at a volume of collected poems, *The Avenue Bearing the Initial of Christ into the*

New World, the title poem quickly becoming his best-known poem and remaining even today one of the most highly regarded by his critics. Kinnell was rewarded the Shelley Prize by the Poetry Society of America, appropriate for his reputation as a leading neoromantic poet.

By the middle of the seventies official signs of Kinnell's achieved status as a poet began to appear. In 1975 he received the Medal of Merit from the National Institute of Arts and Letters. Kinnell has always tended to be a leader, not a follower, among contemporary poets. He was able to promote the reception of poetry through public reading, organizing a reading of a large work by an eighteenth-century poet he had always admired, Christopher Smart's *Jubilate Agno,* including as readers, poets James Wright, Allen Ginsberg, Muriel Rukeyser, and Philip Levine. The revised edition of *Poems of François Villon* in 1977 certified his prestige among American poet translators of French poets as second only to Richard Wilbur's.

Kinnell journeyed abroad again in the late 1970s. He served as Fulbright professor at the University of Nice on the French Riviera, and his relevant book of collected interviews, *Walking Down the Stairs,* the best guide to his poetic intentions, was published by the University of Michigan Press. The next year, 1979, he was a visiting writer at MacQuarrie University in Sydney, Australia. He lingered for a while in the Pacific, living in Hawaii from 1979–82. *Mortal Acts, Mortal Words* was published in 1980. In 1981 Kinnell and Robert Bly sponsored a memorial reading for their friend, the poet James Wright, in New York City. Since there was clearly a need for a one-volume edition of his poems, he selected works from his first six books for *Selected Poems,* published in 1982.

During the eighties, Kinnell's political activities began afresh with a new target: nuclear weapons and nuclear energy. He organized an antinuclear reading, Poets Against the End of the World, at Town Hall, in New York City in 1982. He was now receiving major literary awards and was awarded the Pulitzer Prize for his *Selected Poems* in 1983. He was declared co-winner of the American Book Award the same year. During 1983–84 Kinnell served as president of P. E. N., the international organization of writers. In 1984 he received the largest cash award available to writers, a MacArthur Foundation grant. During 1985 he published his first book of poetry in five years, *The Past,* and he accepted his first tenured academic position as Samuel F. B. Morse Professor of Fine Arts at New York University. His love for Whitman as a poetic predecessor and his critical and scholarly interests in his poetry surfaced again in 1987 with his edition of Whitman's poetry, *The Essential Whitman.* He has become an all but regular contributor of poetry to the *New Yorker* magazine.

What a Poet Knows

In his review of Kinnell's early poetry James Dickey welcomed Kinnell as a poet whose poetry "holds out some promise" largely because of a "necessary involvement" of many of his poems "with the author's life." (Dickey, 135). Dickey was right about the subjectivity. Galway Kinnell's life is consequential for his poems. He has even linked his fictive life in poetry with his actual public life of political commitments in several of his best poems; and, more important, he has written his poetry out of his own experience as a survivor subject to the same mortality as all breathing creatures are. In his poems, typically, his persona seems to be the poet himself. He uses moments associated with real places, but he avoids even the appearance of unfolding any narrative of his life. He gives the impression of being deeply involved in the subjects of his poetry, in the postmodernist mode instead of ironically distancing himself in the best modernist fashion. His poems, when heard, seem to be written for reading to an audience, and in his public appearances Kinnell as reader is perceptibly involved with his poetry. Among contemporary poets, he has the earned reputation of being one of the finest readers of his poetry; actually he is a reciter rather than a reader of the text, much as Robert Frost was a "sayer" of his poems. Along with William Stafford and Sharon Olds, Kinnell appeared as a commentator on poetry and as a powerful reader of his own poetry in a 1990 Bill Moyers educational television special on contemporary poets. The program was singled out for praise by the distinguished television critic John Leonard on the Charles Kuralt Sunday Morning program on CBS. It is evident that when Kinnell reads his poems, before the camera as before audiences, there is much more at hand than the mere reading of words. In all his readings Kinnell pays great attention to the words as if to call attention to the physical things that his words represent.

Like Wallace Stevens, Kinnell can compose a long poem out of serious meditations, building poems on traditional subjects such as time and mortality, in the great tradition of meditative poetry. His poetry is distinctively his own; however, he owes much to those poets who have been liberating forces from too much technology and civilization in modern life and from an excess of formalism and modernism in modern poetry. Donald Hall regards as significant a comment Kinnell made to him: "I have no interest in any poem to which the poet does not bring everything he knows."[4] Included in what a poet should know and bring to poetry would be knowledge of other poets, especially the old masters. Poets who have influenced Kinnell include Whitman, Yeats, and Rilke among earlier poets; among later poets, Ezra Pound, Theodore Roethke, Charles Olson and Allen Ginsberg, all poetic gurus of postmodernism. Kinnell is acquainted with his contemporaries, but he has always believed that for him they are a lesser influence. His forte has never been the irony of modernism, "the satiric intensity" that Yeats designated for the modern poet. Rather, a reading of his poems will reveal that he is personal and more engaged in the postmodernist mode. His poems reflect his grasp of his own existential situation as a man and a poet. Kinnell has proclaimed: "I know I live half alive in the world; I know half my life belongs to the wild darkness" (*FH*, 46). His poetry is based on an empathy for all things that live and must die. Throughout his poems there is a pervading feeling of the mortality, not just of the poet, but of all things. He has summed up much of his credo as a poet and the essence of his poems:

> If the things and creatures that live on earth don't possess mystery, then there isn't any. To touch this mystery requires, I think, love of the things and creatures that surround us: the capacity to go out to them so that they enter us, so that they are transformed within us, and so that our own inner life finds expression through them. (*WDS*, 52)

It will be quickly evident that Galway Kinnell's career as a poet is not one from which a survey can facilely distinguish periods or even trace thematic development. As a poet he simply plays a relatively small number of variations on a few major concerns. The best introduction to Galway Kinnell as a poet would be his own commentary in his published interviews and in his own critical essays, discussed in the next chapter. His criticism is not extensive, but it is exceptional commentary on his own poetry.

Chapter Two

The Poetic Milieu of Galway Kinnell: From Modernism to Postmodernism and Neoromanticism

A Time of Transition

Born in 1927, Galway Kinnell was one of a generation of American poets who were trying to establish themselves as published poets at a time when the modernist practice in poetry and the formalist New Criticism theory, in vogue during their college years, had come under attack. It is important to see his poetry in the context of the transition that was taking place when he began writing from modernism to postmodernism. Four decisive events that signified change in the 1950s were the appearance of Charles Olson's antiformalist *Projective Verse* manifesto in 1950; the publication of Philip Larkin's personal poetry in *Poems* in England in 1954; the sensationalism of Allen Ginsberg's Beat protest poem *Howl* in 1956; and the impact of Robert Lowell's apparently confessional *Life Studies* in 1959. By the late 1950s and the early 1960s Allen Ginsberg and Gary Snyder were gurus for the Beat Movement; Robert Bly, James Wright, and Louis Simpson were exemplars for the Deep Image Movement; Charles Olson, Robert Creeley, and Robert Duncan were supporters of a movement away from formalism to freer, open forms in poetry. These poets were clearly becoming the new generation of poets in the late 1950s and early 1960s. Robert Lowell, Randall Jarrell, and John Berryman, a decade older, were designated as "Middle-Generation" poets who were now busily restructuring their previous modernist ironic mode and impersonal poetic personae. For the lack of a more precise name, *postmodernism* was the term soon fashioned by critics to depict new directions in poetry. It was a time when the pendulum had perceptibly swung away from the professed antiromanticism of Eliot and formalist practice of the New Criticism to a new fashion of neoromantic exploration and self-discovery in theme and in technique.

The modernist theories targeted by this critical restyling were the formalist theory of T. S. Eliot, identifying poetry as autotelic and impersonal, with poets ideally finding "objective correlatives" for their personal feelings; and the formalist New Criticism of the 1940s which instructed readers how to read and poets how to write poems in the ambiguous and ironic modernist style. The late 1950s and early 1960s are the most convincing dates for a watershed moment for the beginning of the decline of modernism and formalism. There was a reaction to the overemphasis on poetry as a craft and the poem as linguistic artifact. It was a time for rejoinders in critical theory and in poetic practice to a prevailing view that modern poetry belonged in the traditions of seventeenth-century metaphysical poetry with its irony and wit, and of nineteenth-century symbolism with its emphasis on private symbols and its taste for myth.

Behind modernistic critical theories had been a cultural attitude towards history which found, in Eliot's language, a "chaos and anarchy" in modern times, contrasting sharply with the accepted and meaningful rituals characteristic of a more traditional past. Juxtaposition of past and present in Joyce's *Ulysses* or in Eliot's *The Waste Land* was designated by Eliot as the "Mythical Method." Monroe K. Spears, in a valuable interpretation, has found the outstanding characteristic of modernism to be various forms of discontinuity—between the present and the accepted values of the past, between the poet hiding behind the mask of his persona and his poem as artifact, and within the poem, a chaos of form to reflect an age in chaos.[1]

The main targets of postmodernist practice were the modernist doctrines that the persona in the poem has to be divorced from the poet and that a poem is an art object that distances itself from life. Reacting to the modernist assumption that the poet creates a persona, the postmodernists of the 1960s took the view that the speaker should be perceived as the poet. The reader is no longer to presuppose that the *I* is an invented character. In their extremely personal confessional poetry, Robert Lowell, Anne Sexton, and Sylvia Plath wrote about personal afflictions which would ordinarily have been reserved for private communication to an analyst.

Commenting on the dominant mood of the last 25 years of postmodernism, David Perkins determines that the "salient characteristics of contemporary American poetry are, in general, that it is or seems spontaneous, personal, naturalistic, open in form and antagonistic to the idea of form, intellectually skeptical yet morally concerned and sometimes even righteous, and imbued with feelings of vulnerability, yet with the humor of resignation, acknowledging helplessness."[2] Clearly, any aesthetic distance from personal revelation provided by irony is gone. Recognizing this change, Perkins identifies the two conspicuous traits of postmodernist poetry in this manner: the poem appears to be personal and it gives also the semblance of spontaneous speech. With some recent poets there has been a further reaction against the view of poetry as artifact through an attempt to recapture the mythologizing mind of primitive peoples. In the 1960s the attitudes of many poets became simultaneously personal and political with the outbreak of social protest from concern over nuclear arms, segregation, Vietnam.

Postmodernism and Open Forms

If the poet has been returned to poetry, what then are the major structural forms of the postmodernist poetry of the last 30 years? David Perkins identifies the forms of recent poetry as a mixture of the old and the new, with a preference for the freer forms: "traditional and free verse in narrative, dramatic monologue, long meditation, list, catalogue, and lyric, including sonnet, song, chant, litany, spell, and mantra." (Perkins, 345). Galway Kinnell's own work began as relatively formal and structurally intricate poems, but he soon moved to a simpler diction, to a looser line, and to an overall freer structure. He has tried to write lyrics sustaining a music that stays true to the inner shape of the poem but never venturing too far from a sense of the speaking voice. Among literary historians there has always been some uncertainty as to whether postmodernism has attempted to nullify modernism completely or to carry it on to a more radical stage. In the fifties and sixties poets like Charles Olson, Robert Creeley, and Robert Duncan may have thought that they were only carrying the poetic revolution begun about 1910 forward to another stage of development. The early poetic work of Ezra Pound and William Carlos Williams provided the specific models for what they were attempting. Even though a postmodernist, Kinnell probably had little feel of participating in a recognizable postmodernist rebellion. By the time he began publishing, the irony, wit, and impersonality characteristic of modernist practice and justified by new critical theory had simply passed out of fashion. Kinnell's poetry evidences this passing. One of the passages that David Perkins uses in his definitive history of modern poetry to illustrate the transformation that had taken place in American poetry is fittingly taken from "Little Sleep's-Head Sprouting Hair," in Kinnell's *Book of Nightmares* (1971).

> learn to reach deeper
> into the sorrows
> to come—to touch
> the almost imaginary bones
> under the face, to hear under the laughter
> the wind crying across the black stones. Kiss
> the mouth
> which tells you, ***here,***
> ***here is the word.*** This mouth. This laughter. These
> temple bones. (*BN,* 52)

Kinnell as Neoromantic

Perkins's point is well made that verse like this by Kinnell could not have been written earlier, in the 1940s and early 1950s. It is not entirely the poet; it is also the age that makes the poetry. Galway Kinnell is a postmodernist poet of importance and almost as distinctive a stylist as James Dickey. Kinnell's style was always a bit too personal and too romantic for the modernist taste of the fifties, more a new poetry of the sixties rather than the old poetry of the fifties and the forties. If it means anything to call him a neoromantic, it at least underscores his fascination with death. If Kinnell were a religious poet more inclined to traditional mythology, it would be easy to describe his concern mythically as a fascination with the journey to death, a kind of symbolic descent into hell, with a possible resurrection; but his stress is even closer to a more basic and more primitive one on death as a return to a preconscious or prehuman state. Kinnell's version of the myth is primitive and pre-Christian, simply emphasizing the individual's participation in a natural and universal process. It also owes something to a romantic "one life" belief that our deepest desire is "to be one with all creation" and for transgressions requiring a propitiatory act. Kinnell shares with James Dickey a fascination with imagining the conscious mind reuniting with its unconscious underpinnings, with the human vision regaining a way of seeing characteristic of the nonhuman. There is, however, a difference in scale. If Dickey would like to become the sea gull he empathizes with both in his poetry and in his prose, Galway Kinnell would become one with the more corporeal bear he imagines in his poetry.

Galway Kinnell's usual method of discerning our sameness with everyone and with everything is by delving more deeply into himself, not just into any better self, but even into his worst self, discovering in the process that what he had thought was personal is in fact universal. He is interested in inciting primitive archetypes, "the archaic and primitive ritual dramas," in order to minister to the fissures in the psyche of modern man. Kinnell is best treated as a postmodernist neoromantic, but he still has a modernist concern with at least hinting at the creation of myth in his poetry and echoing Eliot's alarm over a dissociation of sensibility, the old Cartesian split between thought and feeling, from which both modern poet and modern man suffer.

In his attitude towards death Kinnell actually turns out to be as much realist as romantic. He faces death, as Emily Dickinson did, and as Robert Frost did not, with only the hope of the continuity of life left to mediate the thought of death, acknowledging there is nothing that can resurrect the dead. For in Kinnell's poetry the traditional theme of the continuity of life cannot adequately compensate for an individual death, such as his brother's death remembered in several poems, most poignantly in the elegy "Freedom, New Hampshire":

> But an incarnation is in particular flesh
> And the dust that is swirled into a shape
> And crumbles and is swirled again had but one shape
> That was this man. When he is dead the grass
> Heals what he suffered, but he remains dead
> And the few who loved him know this until they die. (*WKIW,* 61)

The only compensation for Kinnell is that dying may be an entrance into the mystery, a return to the unconscious and the preconscious; but this possibility can never quite compensate for loss of identity, for the death of the conscious self. Kinnell comprehends death as well as other matters in his poetry often in terms of what poststructuralist criticism identifies as "binary oppositions," with pain and fear as strongly felt as any compensating faith can be. I find little specific evidence that he consciously utilizes the depth psychology myths of Carl Gustav Jung, much read in the 1950s; but he does believe that we must face something like the Jungian shadow, involving the unconscious and the forces of primitive darkness, before any regeneration or return to psychic health. The most positive gain possible for humankind in his poetry is the wonder and awe that come from a grasping of the wholeness and oneness of life. He writes in his essay "Poetry, Personality, and Death": "The death of the self I seek, in poetry and out of poetry, is not a drying up or withering. It is a death, yes, but a death out of which one might hope to be reborn more giving, more alive, more open, more related to the natural life" (*PPD,* 222). Kinnell clearly rejects the mysticism of Eastern Buddhism with its aspiration to be purged of fleshly desire. He is concerned with physicality, and he envisions a death that would impart "greater desire, not less".

As a poet Galway Kinnell is in the tradition of the poetry of empathy of Whitman, and more recently, that of the actual exchange of identity of James Dickey. He writes in admiration of Whitman:

> It's one of the things that makes "Song of Myself" glorious. As we read this poem, we have to open ourselves if we are to get anything at all out of it. When we come to the lines "I was the man, I suffered, I was there," we already understand what it is to disappear into someone else. The final action of the poem, where Whitman dissolves into the air and into the ground, is for me one of the great moments of self-transcendence in poetry. (*WDS,* 22–23)

Kinnell calls his version of Whitmanesque empathy a feeling of "kinship," and, influenced by the French existentialism of the fifties, even identifies it as "a terrible kinship." It is terrible because it requires a loss of identity and the death of the self. With such preoccupations Kinnell might seem to be fixedly a morbid and death-obsessed poet, one whose preoccupations are with "the relation of the self to violence, transience, and death." But to him death actually has a dual meaning. It is "the flowing away into the universe, which we desire" (*PPD,* 209), as well as the extinction, which we fear. Whitman, as a nineteenth-century romantic, sees death as the greatest moment; Kinnell, as a twentieth-century neoromantic, accepts it more realistically as an "insoluble moment."

James Dickey cherishes the Biblical word *beheld* and uses it to indicate a new, more intense way of seeing things. Kinnell does not use this exact word, but he definitely wants to catch some of the same sense of seeing more intensely one's relationship to nature and to things in this world in the manner that Dickey denoted with his use of the word *beheld.*

Kinnell is aware that his view of death differs from that of many twentieth-century poets. Charles Molesworth suggests that the line most critical of Frost in Kinnell's fine poem "For Robert Frost" is that the older poet was "not fully convinced that he was dying."[3] He writes, "a man, what shall I say, / Vain, not full convinced he was dying . . ." (*FH,* 25). The perspective of Kinnell's persona, unlike Frost's, must constantly include an awareness that he is dying, for the process of living is also dying; "burning" is his favorite metaphor. There is a key statement in his essay "The Poetics of the Physical World": "The poetics of heaven agrees to the denigration of pain and death; in the poetics of the physical world these are the very elements" (*PPW,* 119). Kinnell's poetry embraces a physical world that requires an awareness of the relentless ongoing of time and accepts the "denigration of pain and death."

Kinnell also records in "The Poetics of the Physical World": "Of course, the desire to be some other thing is itself suicidal, involving as it must a willingness to cease to be a man, to be extinct" (*PPW,* 123). But this is only one half of Kinnell's message; he does not have a simple wish for extinction so much as he has a complex urge for a union with what is also loved. His desire is for more, not less life.

Benjamin De Mott once relegated James Dickey to what he called "the 'more life' school" of poetry.[4] The same simplistic classification could be fashioned, with more justification, for Kinnell. Charles Molesworth equates what Kinnell was trying to do with what Theodore Roethke had sought to accomplish in his poetry, even quoting Roethke in "Open Letter," published posthumously in *On the Poet and his Craft.* Molesworth relates of Kinnell: "He must scorn being "mysterious" or loosely oracular, but be willing to face up to a genuine mystery. His language must be compelling and immediate; he must create an actuality" (Molesworth, 102).

Molesworth also warns of a danger in Kinnell's poetry: he risks being either sentimental or "loosely oracular" when he rejects irony. He is successful only when he achieves "the immersion of empathy" (*Molesworth,* 104). Kinnell is aware of the risk of being "loosely oracular"; and, if he is truly a neoromantic, he nevertheless has a very unromantic belief that the ego hinders true poetry if a poet cannot go beyond mere solipsism. The poet supplies a need all of us have. We need to come to terms with ourselves and with our natural environment. At its best there is a terrible honesty in most postmodernist poetry. This honesty is a characteristic of Galway Kinnell's best poetry. To be convincing Kinnell often goes in his poetry from words to expressive gestures and on to symbolic acts.

Although it is easy to recognize Galway Kinnell as an important postmodernist poet, it is extremely difficult to categorize his style. He certainly cannot be simply pigeonholed—any more than James Dickey can—as a Black Mountain poet, a New York poet, a Beat poet, or a San Francisco poet. Perkins includes him with poets he describes as "against civilization," with an atoning interest in myth and archetypal symbol, with such poets as Robert Bly, W. S. Merwin, Gary Snyder, and Louise Glück. These poets share with the surrealists an impulse to escape from the limitations of a personal voice and of naturalistic immediacy, to speak from a "deeper, more universal level of feeling and experience" (Perkins, 559–60); and they often focus their poems on dreams. Kinnell and these poetic colleagues are neoromantics who oppose civilization by promoting a return to nature and to primitive conditions without any compensating romantic delusions that this state is necessarily better than the civilized state. Nature is perceived as the wilderness, specifically, as the trails of the West by Gary Snyder, or the farm country of Minnesota by Robert Bly; or the wilderness is depicted as the scene in interactions between people and animals in Kinnell's poetry. To all these poets, certainly including Galway Kinnell, nature is the unconscious as opposed to the conscious mind.

The Anxiety of Influences

Granted Galway Kinnell's poetry initiates in a poetic milieu that marked a change in literary styles from modernism to postmodernism, there remains the question of what older established and peer poets he read in the fifties were specific influences on his poetry. At Princeton his early enthusiasm was for the great modernist Yeats, which fellow student poet W. S. Merwin shared. Yeats was the textbook example then of a great modern poet. Later came an enthusiasm for Walt Whitman and Emily Dickinson, whose reputations were being established in the fifties as nineteenth-century poets who were, nevertheless, modern in significant though different ways. This decade welcomed, at long last, a good edition of Dickinson's poetry and sympathetic studies of Whitman as the first great American modernist. In the 1950s both were being reread from a twentieth-century perspective, and in new and better editions of their poetry. For Kinnell, after these influences, with his knowledge of the language, there was the attraction of the French symbolists and postsymbolists poets that he read extensively while he was on a Fulbright in France. In philosophy the existentialism of Jean-Paul Sartre and Albert Camus, a strong influence in America in the fifties, was undoubtedly reinforced by his sojourn in France. Kinnell's early published poems clearly reflect the "God is dead" existentialism of the time since God is acutely absent from his poetic cosmos. There is much *weltschmerz* about this in Kinnell's poems, which probably comes from his somewhat later reading of Rilke, who is certainly a major influence and whom Kinnell regards as the greatest poet of the twentieth century, even above Yeats.

The movement in Kinnell's own poetry towards freer and looser poems undoubtedly results in part from the influence by a radical movement of which he became an observer—the open forms philosophy of Charles Olson and the Black Mountain poets, whose quarters he inhabited the summer before his graduation at Princeton. He soon abandoned stanzas and meters for free verse, his early penchant for romantic diction for a more contemporary speech.

Existentially, as a seriously thinking poet in the fifties, Galway Kinnell wanted to show that he too had ultimate concern (so much admired at the time) about poetry and about life. The influence remained after the passing of the decade. He has achieved this goal of gravity almost to his detriment. About these matters Kinnell has been his own spokesman often in his poetry but also in his prose.

Chapter Three
The Prose of a Poet

Through the Mirror of Subjective Criticism: Kinnell and the Interview

A reading of Galway Kinnell's prose—his critical essays, especially his interviews, his novel—definitely furthers an understanding of his poetry. His essays and the interviews perceivably register the concerns of the poems. The most important prose document is the major collection of interviews, *Walking Down the Stairs.*[1] This book is the best place to begin for an understanding of his poetry.

An essential critical stance of postmodernism is to disregard Eliot's modernist dictum about impersonality through making subjective statements about one's poetry. Though *Walking Down the Stairs* is less sensational than the *Self-Interviews* of James Dickey, it is an important postmodernist document. Randall Jarrell's volume *Poetry and the Age* was an influential precursor in the fifties of the interviews and self-interviews of poets in the sixties and seventies because it was audaciously personal for 1952, replete with impressionistic and subjective judgments by a poet critic.[2] Reading Jarrell in the fifties led many students of literature to turn against what they came to look upon as the arid formalism of the New Criticism. In the sixties, as the poetry critic for the *Sewanee Review,* James Dickey revealed his own personal likes and dislikes and equated the sort of poetry he was writing with the kind of poetry he approved of as a critic. By the early seventies Dickey introduced in a book of tape-recorded interviews a new form of postmodernist criticism, his self-interview.[3]

Kinnell is more unassuming than Dickey, but he acquiesces to the interview as a form of literary criticism in which a poet uses his own poetry for comments on the situation of modern poetry and his own relationship to that situation. He has embraced the interview as a means of conveying his own views of what he has written; but, more modestly than Dickey, he accepts the New Critical doctrine that the poet has no special advantages in interpreting his own work. He even concurs with some of the other doctrines of the New Critics, admitting in his preface to *Walking Down the Stairs* that he believes in the relativism of the intentional fallacy, so important to formalist theory, in that it is a fallacy to believe that "there is a key to every poem and the author has it . . . I happen to think that the author may be the last one to know what his work is about" (*WDS,* ix). Within these restrictions, Kinnell is quite willing to have his own say about what he has written and to declare his own critical beliefs. He accepts the basic New Critical doctrine that form and content are not separable entities. It is his understanding that "there is no such thing as technique . . . apart from the poems that use it" (*WDS,* ix).

Since Galway Kinnell has written only a small number of critical essays, his major contribution to literary criticism and his major prose commentary on his own work would be the interviews in *Walking Down the Stairs.* I have selected several topics to introduce Kinnell as a poet-critic, and which will allow for a personal poet-guided introduction to Kinnell's poetry.

A Concern with Animals

Critics have concurred that, although he has written a few imposing urban poems, Galway Kinnell is basically a nature poet who has written some of the finest contemporary poems about animals—among them a porcupine, a crow, various bears, a sow or two—producing a kind of minor bestiary. Animals are, he makes it clear, important in his poetry for revealing an unsuspected kinship, suggesting, if not proposing, a mythology of the common fate of living things. In response to a question about the frequent recurrence of animal imagery in his poetry, Kinnell replied: "Yes, there are many animals in my poems. I've wanted to see them in themselves and also to see their closeness to us. I don't think I've succeeded in creating a mythology in my poetry, but I know it's the dream of every poem to be a myth" (*WDS,* 5).

Kinnell shares with James Dickey a desire for the empathy of immersion, to enter imaginatively and sympathetically into another creature's life. In "The Bear," one of Galway's most celebrated animal poems, the person speaking actually enters the animal's body physically, not just in the chastity of his imagination. Kinnell acknowledges his regard for animals in his poems as part of his tribute "to the things and creatures that share the world with us" (*WDS,* 61). His intention is to show that "their closeness to us" proceeds from this common sharing. He may not have intended to create a mythology, but there is clearly the seed for a bestiary myth.

The Craft of Poetry

Since formalist critics stressed poetry as a craft, there was a widespread belief when Galway Kinnell was a student that criticism—as then taught at Iowa, Yale, Kenyon, Minnesota, Indiana, and his own Princeton—was something important for writers to learn. The craft of poetry was something to be taught like any other literary subject; many young poets of the fifties generation would take writing courses at a university (Iowa was the popular choice) where New Critical ideas prevailed to learn to write the "well-made poem" according to the convictions of the New Critics. Before a poet experimented away from form, there was a firm belief that he or she must first master form. Here Kinnell responds to a question on the formalism of his generation of poets: "That was what happened to my generation. Almost all of us begin writing in strict forms. Almost all of us sooner or later turned to free verse" (*WDS,* 18–19).

Atypically for a writer of his generation, Kinnell has always been skeptical that formal writing courses could help one become a poet. He never bothered to take the fashionable writing courses at Princeton taught by the eminent critic R. P. Blackmur and by the poet-in-residence John Berryman. He even felt a "certain scorn that there could be a course in poetry" (*WDS,* 9). He preferred learning his craft as a young poet by trial and hard work, simply showing his poems to one chosen mentor, a more experienced writer and teacher he respected, and he continued this relationship for many years. "I had one teacher to whom I showed my poems, the poet Charles Bell. He helped and encouraged me a great deal. He remains my closest friend and the person to whom I send my poems when I first write them" (*WDS,* 9). Kinnell regards himself as principally a poet not a novelist, though he has written one novel. He states succinctly the problem of writing another novel. "Life is short, however, and novels are long" (*WDS,* 40). The main difference between writing novels and poetry is that as a novelist he has to conceive of "a world outside myself, one populated by other beings, who are in relationship with each other"

(*WDS,* 6). By contrast a poem "is mostly an inner world." Kinnell's poems may be populated by other living creatures, such as animals; but they are, aside from his relatively recent family poems, much more rarely populated by other human beings. His poems can be as solitary, because of the absence of others, as Emily Dickinson's.

A further distinguishing characteristic of Kinnell's poetry is that he has not thoroughly bought the doctrine that a poem must have some of the narrative appeal of the short story and the immediacy of an apparently confessional performance in which the person seems clearly to be the poet himself—something which other postmodernist poets such as Robert Lowell, Anne Sexton, and Sylvia Plath, subscribed to in the confessional sixties. In his view the basic form of poetry is still the lyric, an appropriate medium for the initial purpose of describing the inner world. A poem starts out being about one's self as "a fragment of autobiography" but then it must also "go deeper than personality" (*WDS,* 6). The voice the reader hears in his poems is a personal voice, but Kinnell believes that it also must be one that in the end "takes on that strange voice, intensely personal yet common to everyone." The private feelings that his poems express must turn out to be "the feelings of everyone else as well" (*WDS,* 6). Although an important perspective of the postmodernist movement in poetry was the autobiographical anguish in the confessional poetry of Robert Lowell, Anne Sexton, Sylvia Plath, and John Berryman, Kinnell never becomes personally confessional because what should be heard is not the confessional voice of the poet but rather one through which "all rituals are spoken . . . The separate egos vanish. The poem becomes simply the voice of a creature on earth speaking" (*WDS,* 6).

In a recent interview Kinnell seems to express both a romantic faith in organic form, that being a view of the poem "writing" itself—a process that goes beyond the intentions of the poet—and a formalist belief that out of the struggle with form there comes, in the most meaningful poems, the adventure of discovery.

> I think I generally know the subject of the poem, but I don't know where it will go. I have an idea of how long it will be. I don't know why I know that. But that's about all I know, the subject and the length. I think if I did know how it was going to come out, I would be less interested in writing it, because the discovery, the hope of discovery, is often frustrated. (*BWR,* 171)

In the same recent interview Kinnell hedges in theory, as he does in practice, between the discipline of form and the liberties of free verse. He believes that the "new formalists" among contemporary poets are leading a return to form with a flexible metrics. His own practice has shown him that rhyme and to a lesser degree even metre "impose such restrictions on the way you can say something, and even dictate what you can say, what you must say, that other difficulties in writing, that is, the difficulties of knowing, can't be truly faced" (*BWR,* 179–80). Nevertheless, these experimentations with a return to form have instructed him and other poets that free verse can become too prosaic; this has created a wide dissatisfaction with the way such verse "is widely practiced." The use of free verse does not mean that there should be "no formal character at all" to the poetry (*BWR,* 180).

The Common Humanity of the Poet

Galway Kinnell perceptibly thinks of himself as a nature poet though he has written urban poems and even more public, sociological and political poems. Though a political activist in his opposition to segregation in the South, to the war in Vietnam, and to the development and use of nuclear weapons, he has always been more of a nature poet than a political poet. Critical consensus acknowledges that Kinnell has written at least three major political poems, "Vapor Trail Reflected in the Frog Pond," "The Dead Shall be Raised Incorruptible," and "The Fundamental Project of Technology," which should be ranked among the best political poems of the last quarter of a century. In his own comments on politics and poetry, Kinnell makes the point that the major reason for writing political poetry is a common humanity: "I doubt if poetry can come from a person who feels nothing for others, who can't imagine someone else's sufferings" (*WDS,* 17). Nevertheless, he has repeatedly stated his preference for nature poems. In *Walking Down the Stairs* he muses:

> The idea that we and our creations don't belong to "nature" comes from the notion that the human being is a special being created in God's image to have dominion over all else. We are becoming aware of our connection with other beings. That's hopeful since for several centuries our civilization has done all it could to forget it. (*WDS,* 17)

Galway Kinnell is also genuinely concerned with a problem that has bothered poets since the romantic era, the dissociation of sensibility—in intellectual history sometimes called "the Cartesian split" between logic and emotion, with the former regarded as the only viable means of per-

ception. He understands this split from the perspective of a neoromantic who appreciates the imaginative apprehension of nature and that of a twentieth-century outdoors man who loves physical contact with nature. We have lost any feeling for fraternity with the other living creatures in nature. He esteems Henry David Thoreau as "a new man we have yet to catch up with, who sickens in the presence of the will to detach, objectify, dominate." In his poetry Kinnell would be such a man. He is a poet who offers his own distinctive version of the modern world as a place in which man is out of balance, dominated both by a desire for power and the tyranny of reason.

Not surprisingly for a poet who is concerned thematically with the acts of "hunting, cultivation, propitiation," Kinnell explicitly believes that all good writing must be experiential, based on actual experience: "My poetry does stay fairly close to the experiences of my life." He does not easily find objective correlatives, and he does not sanction objective forms like the dramatic monologue. "I don't usually write in others' voices" (*WDS*, 18). But he never goes so far as to celebrate unadulterated individuality. Instead he characteristically considers that life is not unique but much the same as others' lives—situated in a kind of great chain of being. His poetry is written from that perspective.

> The best poems are those in which you are not this or that person, but anyone, just a person. If you could go further, you would not be a person but an animal. If you went further still, you would be the grass, eventually a stone. If a stone could speak your poem would be its words. (*WDS*, 23)

Kinnell is concerned that for many readers his poetry may seem to have a kind of death obsession. He agrees that many of his poems may appear obsessively death concerned. As a commentator on his own poetry, he would like to make his view clear regarding this subject: death is not conclusively a finality but rather a tacit continuation in some other form. He points out in a passage crucial to his poetry: "Yes, as death has two aspects—the extinction which we fear, and the flowing away into the universe which we desire—there is a conflict within us that I want to deal with" (*WDS*, 23). It is out of this conflict that the drama of much of Kinnell's poetry originates.

There is a difference of opinion among Kinnell's critics as to whether he avers the opportunity for transcendence in the world of his poetry. He admires transcendence in Whitman's poetry and yearns for something akin to it in his own. "One of the great moments of self-transcendence in poetry," Kinnell says, is when Whitman in "Song of Myself" "dissolves into the air and into the ground" (*WDS,* 23). Is there any comparable transcendence achieved in Kinnell's poetry? Lee Zimmerman, for one, fails to find it in the poems he examines.[4] My own reading of Kinnell pretty much confirms Zimmerman's view. There is, as Kinnell admits, "a streak of transcendentalism in all this" (*WDS,* 97); but in his poetry transcendence is actually something that happens not in this world but after death. Kinnell testifies that about halfway through his first book he stopped looking for the traditional kind of transcendence in this world and turned to writing poems about struggles "to be rid of such a desire" in expressly antitranscendental poems (*WDS,* 24). To Kinnell, a person must confront nature on its own and on his own physical terms. He sounds much like James Dickey when he declares that a "poem is a kind of paradigm of what the human being wants to say to the cosmos" (*WDS,* 24–25). Rather than transcend the ordinary he would prefer to reach out to the cosmic level from common, shared experience.

Kinnell is attracted to the nonhuman world as providing "the basic context of human existence." It is in this context, "in the presence of the wind, or the night sky, or the sea," and, he adds, even from the "less spectacular instances of the nonhuman . . . that poetry springs" (*WDS,* 88). He singles out Anne Sexton's poem on the night sky, "The Starry Night," written in response to Vincent Van Gogh's powerful painting, as admirably expressing "both a death wish and yet strangely life-giving" (*WDS,* 88–89).

Kinnell believes that in his own poetry "there has been less autobiography than there seems to be" (WDS, 100). If we read his poems correctly, we see that they may begin with personal experience, with actual autobiography; but they become more universal, seeking to establish a shared experience with others. What is important on this earth is "happiness in this life," although humans are in the very untranscendental situation of having only the capacity to sense this condition. "This makes us able, when our time comes, to die willingly, to return to it without bitterness or the feeling of having been betrayed" (*WDS,* 97–98).

Death and the Poet

Galway Kinnell belongs to a tradition in American poetry that accepts death as an important subject. In addition to his comments in *Walking Down the Stairs,* he has written an essay, "Poetry, Personality and Death" (contributed to *A Field Guide to Contemporary Poetics and Poetry*), specifically on the subject of death and the poet, death and the individual personality.[5] It is a further work basic to the understanding of his poetry. Kinnell's attitude is almost one of gratitude for having found a universal subject that restrains him from being "self-absorbed" and introspective, personal and confessional, as so many of his contemporaries have been. It is a topic that does not allow him to be niggardly interested in his own experience to the exclusion of everybody else's. His perspective is that contemporary poets require subjects that will liberate them from the narrowness of "this self-absorbed, closed ego" that humans are afflicted with. He begins this essay with an account of a man on a bus who cried out, "You don't know how I suffer! No one else on this bus suffers the way I do!" He receives an offer from one passenger, "Do you want to borrow my crutches?" This act should communicate, but Kinnell imagines modern man failing to grasp any sense of suffering and common humanity. On the contrary, what he "would like to find in poetry, as he would on that bus, is one who could express the pain of everyone." He admires James Dickey's apparent personal honesty in his poem "The Firebombing," acknowledging his failure to accept full guilt living after the war in the comforts of suburban life for his own firebombing as a pilot over Japan during World War Two. But Dickey does not go as far as Kinnell would like him to. He faults Dickey for only dramatizing his failure, not adequately confronting it. His poem betrays itself as lacking a true protagonist, with only "someone else invented to bear the onus the poet does not care to take on himself." It is Kinnell's judgment that in our admiration of the scientific spirit, we have come to admire the ability to detach the mind from what it studied and to allow the mind to become pure will, unattached and free. What this "kills is the creative relationship between man and thing" (*PPD,* 209). It is one of the missions of Kinnell's poetry to warn against that danger.

Kinnell even imagines that he can read changes in that register of our character, the American face. In southern California he remembers meeting Americans with these changed faces, willing to "pollute, bulldoze, ravage, lay waste—as long as it made money" (*PPD,* 211). One of the few places left where there are still "efforts to reintegrate ourselves with life" is in poetry. In Ginsberg's Beat poem "Howl" Kinnell finds an attempt to "move toward a poetry in which the poet seeks an inner liberation by going so deeply into himself—to the worst of himself as well as the best—that he suddenly finds he is everyone" (*PPD,* 213). The poets he likes—and the poet he is trying to become himself—are those who take seriously Thoreau's dictum, "Be it life or death, we crave only reality." These are poets who are "willing to face the worst in ourselves," who have accepted the risk "that probing into one's own wretchedness one may just dig up more wretchedness." In his poetry Galway Kinnell wants to be concerned with life, with love, as Whitman was, but with all aspects of one's self, including death. His version of the death of the self "is not a drying up or withering" but a hope of being reborn "more related to the natural life." His business is not with the Buddhist forms of death that would purge us of desire, remove us from our loves, "but a death that would give me more loves, not fewer. And greater desire, not less" (*PPD,* 222). He adds that he sees his poems on death as analogous to the Navajo night-chant, an expression of desire which "gives whoever says it with his whole being, at least for the moment of saying it, and who knows, perhaps forever, everything he asks."

Kinnell on The Anxiety of Influences

Unlike some poets, Galway Kinnell is not reluctant to comment on specific influences on his poetry. His interviews are generous in his acknowledgments. He says that the last section of *The Book of Nightmares* was written in the spirit of Emily Dickinson's "heightened feeling for the world at the moment of death" (*WDS,* 23). Among philosophical influences he admits there lurks the long shadow of Friedrich Hegel. Kinnell is especially taken with what Hegel said on death: "The life of the spirit is not frightened at death and does not keep itself pure of it. It lives with death and maintains itself in it" (*WDS,* 24). This idea recurs in various forms in Kinnell's poetry.

In *Walking Down the Stairs* and in other prose comments, Kinnell not only identifies specific influences on his poetry, but he also helpfully makes clear his own individual differences, even from poets he respects. He admires but still criticizes the godfather of much postmodernist poetry, William Carlos Williams. He concedes that Williams has a concern with things of the physical world that Kinnell can share with him. But he believes that Williams has the limitation of remaining only photographic. He is good at seeing things, but he does not convey to his reader the experience of the thing. "In 'The Red Wheelbarrow' we see the scene but don't experience it" (*WDS,* 37). Things are important for themselves in Williams's poetry, just as they are for Kinnell's own poetry. They are, fortunately, never just symbols for either poet. But what Kinnell seeks transcends the visual image, which Williams is seldom able to do. Kinnell is interested in having things in poetry take on a "shimmering" quality you can feel (*WDS,* 43). He sees but does not feel Williams's things.

Yeats was for Kinnell—as he was to many young poets who read poetry in the fifties—the great modern poet. Yeats seemed even then to be poetry itself, and in everything he wrote early in his career Kinnell made the mistake of simply trying to reproduce not his own but that great poet's distinctive voice. Then, his idea of form as something that does not reveal itself or come together until the end, also came from Yeats. This early influence was initiated by his classmate at Princeton and fellow poet W. S. Merwin reading to him from Yeats's poetry. Later, Kinnell's conception of the persona in poetry became his own, evolving to something that begins out of his own personality and then objectifying as the poem develops until he is enabled to speak in a voice that speaks not just for himself but for others, for his fellow creatures on this earth.

The great German poet Rainer Maria Rilke was unmistakably another influence on Kinnell's poetry. What he liked in Rilke's poetry was the seriousness, the conscious ultimate concern only with subjects that are for him a matter of life and death. Kinnell reports: "He writes at the limit of his powers. There are moments when he seems to write beyond the limit. His poetry gropes out into the inexpressible, like the late music of Beethoven" (*WDS,* 43).

There was nothing trivial in Rilke, no modernist or Eliotian clever commentary; and in like manner there is little of any kind of superficiality in Kinnell's poetry. His original exemplar had been Yeats, but he later came to believe that "Rilke may be the greatest poet of the century" (*WDS,* 84). The Yeatsian influence soon passed, with little residue in the later poetry; the Rilkean influence remains. Kinnell has developed an ability to do his own thing with Rilkean themes and techniques. He is our most Rilkean contemporary poet. A current poet that he could actually share poems with was Denise Levertov, who for a time lived in the same apartment building in New York City. His fellow poet mentor was, then and now, his teacher at Princeton, Charles Bell. He has also accepted advice from his contemporaries, poets John Logan, Robert Bly, and Robert Mezey, without being explicitly influenced. Perhaps a reason Kinnell can discuss influences so freely is that he has a clear sense of his own difference.

Galway Kinnell as Novelist: *Black Light*

Galway Kinnell's most extensive venture into prose is his 1966 novel, *Black Light,* set in Iran in friendlier times. It did not attract a very wide audience of readers then, and it has not been regarded with much critical interest in its own right except as an attempt at the novel form by a writer whose real forte is poetry. It did merit a paperback reissue by North Point Press in 1981, perhaps in part because of the concern with Iran at that time. His experience with the novel may have the additional importance of encouraging a greater interest in point of view and in characterization in his poetry that is apparent beginning with *The Book of Nightmares* in 1971.

The appeal of the novel comes from Kinnell's rather impressive use of realistic detail in depicting a Middle-Eastern world not often explored in Western fiction and from his spinning a tale that is more parable than realistic narrative. It has the added attraction of being a murder story, featuring the vengeance of a father, the old rugmaker Jamshid, taking on the rapist of his daughter. Jamshid's act of protest against the disorder that has entered his ordered world casts him instead into the darkness that is suggested by the "black light" of the title. He is driven into exile, into an effectively imaged surrealistic landscape of a desert. His protagonist becomes as much preoccupied with death as the personae of Kinnell's poems. But each threatening encounter reaffirms in him a passion for life that is implied also in many of the poems but often not expressed as explicitly as it is here. In the end, the father is driven to the walled red-light district of Teheran, where, among the whores, he may commit the incest of lying with his own daughter.

The novel is well written, occasionally even imagistic and poetic, but overall written in a sparser prose style than might have been expected of Kinnell. This spareness may also be a deficiency since the structure is more effectively imparted as much by some rather impressive image patterns as by a spare and functional plot. The most considerable of these images is the bird-of-paradise the old rug weaver is reweaving on his rug at the beginning of the novel. It reappears as the novel progresses as a symbol of Jamshid's growing awareness that life is best known through a knowledge of death and destruction. What one remembers about this novel is that it is with its stylistic virtues and structural defects characteristically what critics would expect of a first novel written by a major poet from his experience of a very different culture. The novel is unusual for an American writer, perhaps our only Iranian novel. It is normally English or European writers who have had experiences of the Middle East, not American poets. For this reason—and as an example of what an American poet is able to do in prose with such foreign experience—*Black Light* remains of interest to readers of Galway Kinnell.

Chapter Four

The Earliest Poems and the First Book

First Poems: 1946–1964

Galway Kinnell's earliest poems, those written about the time of his Princeton days in 1946 and continuing through 1954, were not published until 1970, and then only in a limited edition. They were excluded from his first book of poetry, *What a Kingdom It Was.* In 1974 twenty of his early poems, "out of some hundreds I wrote," were reissued in his first attempt at a collected volume of poems, *The Avenue Bearing the Initial of Christ into the New World, Poems 1946–1964.*[1] The volume also reprinted the poems from his first two books, *What a Kingdom It Was* and *Flower Herding on Mount Monadnock.* Only four of his very early poems—"Two Seasons," "The Feast," "A Winter Sky," "Meditation Among the Tombs"—were picked for his later *Selected Poems,* not published until much later, in 1982. The selection is discriminating; these are credibly the best early poems, but even they give evidence that Kinnell was an accomplished, though a much less powerful poet than he has now become. His judgement of his early work in 1970 was that "those arduous searches for the right iambic beat and the rhyme word seem now like time which could have been better spent." Kinnell clearly wrote these poems in the forties and fifties under the influence of modernist formalist tenets and reread them in the seventies from a later postmodernist perspective.

"Two Seasons," the first of the quartet of early poems included in his selected poems, is a love poem, clearly traditional and unquestionably influenced by his favorite poet at this time—William Butler Yeats. It is a poem of two contrasting seasons, summer and winter, voicing a passion in the summer, and proclaiming in the winter a regret for that momentary passion. The woman in the grip of the first season is "Weary of being mute and undefiled." Then the winter setting is established in the best lines in the poem:

I spoke to you that last winter morning
Watching the wind smoke snow across the ice,
Told how the beauty of your spirit, flesh,
And smile had made day break at night and spring
Burst beauty in the wasting winter's place. (*FP,* 5)

The speaker perceives the regret: "Your eyes replied your worn heart wished it could / Again be white and silent as the snow." The second poem, "The Feast," may well be the best of the early poems. It is a love poem, in which the lovers, lying on the shore, are like the pebbles, wearing themselves back into the sand. The setting is ideal, sunset with the smell of "deer-flesh smoking / On the driftwood fire . . ." (*FP,* 6). If it had not been for their love, they would not have grieved. For love gives them something to lose in death; still if they had not grieved, love would not have survived. In this poem Kinnell has verified what he consistently finds to be the dualities of life, the necessity of sorrow and death as well as the necessity of love and happiness.

"The Feast" is much less obviously indebted to Yeats than the third poem, "A Winter Sky," which is a Yeatsian imitation of the sort that was fairly common in the late forties or in the early fifties. In the former, the two lovers are sitting, again facing the shore, with the woods at their backs. The season, a long and beautiful fall, is passing in spite of the fact that one of the two has wished wistfully: "There may never be an end to fall" (*FP,* 10). A death symptomatic of fall is recorded as one of two ducks "flying away from winter" is dropped by a gun. The other duck flies on into winter without looking back or ever comprehending. Only the human observers grasp that things pass, that life is transient; and the poem ends with an acknowledgement that "winter took fall from the marsh and woods."

The longest poem among these four, "Meditation Among the Tombs," is less effective than the others Kinnell salvaged from the early poems. It is both too long and probably too consciously Yeatsian. It begins in the graveyard tradition with the speaker kneeling on his grave and ends with a dialogue between an old man and youth on the consequences of a choice involving the dangers of birth, a choice "between a living wife" or "a babe delivered safe" (*FP,* 37). It is the only long poem by Kinnell that strangely reminds one of another master of long poems—Edwin Arlington Robinson, who has never been cited as an influence. The old man asks: "Is this a graveyard I am diggin in?" And he notes the coming dawn:

But look, the dawn is lighting up the east,
The clouds are breaking, making way—soon!
Now!—through the dusk comes sliding fast,
Alas, that sullen orange eye, the moon. (*FP,* 38)

His conclusion is that such choices and consequences are part of human existence. "Our ghosts, if such we have, can say at least / We were not misers in our misery."

"A Winter Sky" is a descriptive and mildly meditative poem on mutability; the form it takes is the disbelief of two observers that anything as beautiful as autumn could have an end. The shooting by a fall hunter of one of two ducks, and the accepting, continuing flight of the other into the increasing darkness of winter, lead to an acceptance of winter and of death.

Another poem from *First Poems,* "A Walk in the Country," is interesting because it contrasts the clichés of a "nice summer day"—and the desire to walk in the beauty of such a day—with an awareness of mutability, a coincident perception of the "shortness" of everything.

She said it was nice. It was.
But I could hear only in the close
Green around me and there in the dark
Brown ground I walked on, meadowlark
Or other thing speak sharp of shortness
That makes us all and under like that grass. (*FP,* 6)

An early example of Kinnell's penchant for surrealistic symbolic descriptions of darkness would be the poem "The Comfort of Darkness." In a prehumanistic phase of his poetry, human passion and human love do not compensate for a darkness that sweeps the earth and infects the consciousness of the poet. He tells his companion:

Not even the heat of your blood, nor the pure
Light falling endlessly from you, like rain,
Could stay in my memory there
Or comfort then.
Only the comfort of darkness,
The ice-cold unfreezable brine,
Could melt the cries into silence,
Your bright hands into mine. (*FP,* 8)

"Island of Night" deserves mention as an early example of a poem on Kinnell's later theme of the "burning" destructive power of time. In this poem the speaker dreams of "a beautiful island / Surrounded by an abrasive river and / Gone forever." As he awakens, the compensation is the love that "happened" as "I awoke / and touched you and your eyes opened / Into the river of darkness around us" (*FP,* 7). In "The Feast" Kinnell develops the paradox of the matched nature of love and grief. "The sand turns cold—or the body warms. / If love had not smiled we would never grieve" (*FP,* 10). In "The Glade at Dusk," another constituent of Kinnell's later poetry is introduced, the imagery of blossoming and of the flames of a burning world, a destructiveness with which the poet himself has to identify.

> The glade catches fire, and where
> The birds build nests they brood at evening
> On burning limbs. Spirit of the wood, dream
> Of all who have ever answered in the glade at dusk—
> And grass, grass, blossom through my feet in flames. (*FP,* 21)

Kinnell may have delayed publication of these early poems because he felt that they were demonstrably derivative. These were without doubt poems of the forties and fifties, looking backward at formalist practice. His first collection, *What a Kingdom It Was* (1960), was intended to be more forward looking, a book of the sixties, not the book of the fifties that a collection of his first poems would have made. From the perspective of three decades later, it is possible to see this distinction between the early poems and those he selected to publish at the beginning of the new decade in 1960. But it is also apparent that a few of these early poems, though clearly not in his mature style, also look ahead to the poems of the sixties; whereas some of the later poems of that decade are in many ways perceptibly poems of the fifties. As a collection Kinnell's early poems seem bleak in tone and death-obsessed in theme, just as many of his later books of poetry would seem to his readers. In his early poems, though, this bleakness is compensated for by the more obvious lyrical timbre he intended at that time rather than the tensions of the more dramatic poems he would write later. Not unexpectedly, what is missing is the power that comes from his more mature style. Critics who contend that Kinnell lacks lyric grace should note that he was able to achieve it in his earliest poems, his Yeatsian phase.

Modernism into Postmodernism

What a Kingdom It Was is Galway Kinnell's first significant book of poems, acclaimed by Ralph J. Mills as one of the first books of poetry "signaling decisive changes in the mood and character of American poetry as it departed from the witty, pseudo-mythic verse, apparently written to critical prescription, of the 1950s to arrive at the more authentic, liberated work of the 1960s."[2] What is importantly new in the poetry in Mills's view is that Kinnell is personal, allowing himself to be "thrown back on his own perceptions," without the added ironic vision of the then currently fashionable modernist poetry. The poems are also neoromantic in that the poet is drawn to and involved with the natural world as the scene of his imaginative meditations.

Eight of the poems in this first book were reprinted in his *Selected Poems* (1982): "First Song," "To Christ our Lord," "Westport," "For William Carlos Williams," "The Supper after the Last," "The Schoolhouse," "Freedom, New Hampshire," and "The Avenue Bearing the Initial of Christ into the New World." This is a good selection, but Kinnell leaves out several poems of almost equal merit as if perhaps to suggest that he no longer values this book as much as some of his later ones. It does contain the poem most often identified as by Kinnell. That poem which earned instant attention from reviewers was "The Avenue Bearing the Initial of Christ into the New World." It was a rarity for the time, a successful urban poem. The establishment poet Louise Bogan marvelled how Kinnell was able to write about destitute life in a city slum without sinking into the trap of sentimentality.[3] Another reviewer, James Dickey, from his perspective as poetry editor of the *Sewanee Review,* hinted that this poem might, just might mark a beginning of "the Wave of the Future" (Dickey, 135).

Ralph J. Mills may be correct in finding *What a Kingdom It Was* to be a step away from modernism and its distinctive ironic discourse, but it would not be accurate to regard this book as taking many strides towards a looser postmodernist form. The poems in this first book were, almost without exception, more regular in form than his later poems, which have become slowly but progressively freer in form. The poetry is identifiably Kinnell's, but at the same time still recognizably representative of the fashion of the fifties. Behind the craft of the early poetry there remains an apparent attention to the formalist strictures of the New Criticism and an awareness of the proper traditions for modern poetry identified in

Cleanth Brooks's still influential *Modern Poetry and the Tradition,* dutifully read by English majors and graduate students of that time.[4]

Existentialism and Stoicism

I would suggest a second influence on Kinnell's early poetry, which is also more consonant with the fifties than Ralph J. Mills grants for this poetry. The fifties were also a time of esteem for the French existentialism articulated by Jean-Paul Sartre and Albert Camus which accepted a post-naturalistic view of a hostile, at best, uncaring, and at its worst, senseless, absurd world. The existentialists believed in the terrible freedom of being thrown back on their own perceptions of the world, underscoring the human glory and curse of having to make choices that could alone disclose any possibility of discerning meaning in that world. I stress the influence of existentialism because it was in the intellectual air and because Galway Kinnell had the special advantage of living in France at the time of the greatest fame of the two leading practitioners, Camus and Sartre. Their regard was for existential matters of ultimate concern; this attitude is mirrored in Galway Kinnell's early poetry, with matters often beyond the ordinary.

Anyone apprised of the philosophy and literature of this period was also aware of two divergent existentialisms, Christian and atheistic. In the former, one chooses to make "a leap of faith" to believe what may be logically absurd. In contrast, the non-Christian or atheistic existentialists—Sartre and Camus among them—disclaimed any religious solace, and represented man as alone and cut off from any supernatural adjuncts. Even in his earliest poems Galway Kinnell clearly disavows the Christian version. He is intellectually, if not always emotionally, one with the French existentialists.

It is a truism of contemporary literary scholarship that when Christianity fails for modern writers, the first fallback position has been a version of stoicism. A favorite parable in the fifties was the myth of Sisyphus, who defied his sentence of having the stone he had rolled up the hill roll back down by obstinately pushing it back up again. Lee Zimmerman has remarked that Kinnell's poetry is surprisingly unsuffering, even "severely unstoical" regarding the existential pains modern man suffers. This is certainly an accurate description of the tone of the poems in his first volume, as well as in much of his later poetry (Zimmerman, 171). There is characteristically an acknowledged pain in Kinnell's poetry which is coupled with a recognition of this being a condition humans share with all the other creatures of nature. The resolution of conflict involves the discovery of this kinship with all living things through empathy, leading to a better understanding of the necessity of pain and mortality on the part of the only creature, a human being, who mistakenly thought he might transcend all this. Whatever they may wish, Kinnell's personae cannot totally transcend their pain. The only escape from people's loneliness and separation is precisely their discovery of kinship and identity through experiences they come to realize that they share with all creatures. Kinnell is unrelenting in facing the naturalistic truth that a human being is neither separate from other creations and ultimately superior, nor capable of any lasting transcendent evasion of his or her fate. Rejecting transcendentalism, Kinnell's speakers can be assured only of the physical presence in nature of things which impinge directly on the human consciousness. His poems focus intensely on the consequences of this constant impingement of these other-than-human forces on human life, without acknowledging any transcendent escape from this reality. Galway Kinnell's constant message includes the lesson that people's "lech for transcendence" is an illusion which they must learn to live without.

Almost everyone who has written on Kinnell has been aware of his belief that Christianity is one of the escapes the modern poet must do without. As much as is possible, the modern poet must write without any faith in systems, even though the language of Christianity may remain with him as part of his cultural heritage. The poems in Kinnell's first book are credibly a product of the malaise of the fifties in which they were written. It should be recalled that Kinnell wrote them at a time when God's absence, perhaps even the death of God, was being discussed in theology and contemplated in poetry. The consequence for Kinnell as poet was, as David Perkins has stated, "God was absent from his cosmos but not from his emotions" (Perkins, 575). Kinnell has recently confirmed this judgment: "Of course I was raised as a very devout Christian, and I believed very much in God, so the word God has a resonance for me that can never be taken away" (*BWR,* 175). Nevertheless, Kinnell's posture on this question of God's absence has remained continually consistent throughout his poetry of the sixties and seventies, provoking the orthodox Christian poet Donald Davie into objections that developed into a controversy with Ralph J. Mills over Kinnell's negativism.[5] Davie was offended by what he regarded as Kinnell's disrespect for and his "great play" with "Jesus" or "Christ." What Kinnell's poetry consequently lacked, in Davie's view, were the traditions and disciplines of Christian worship—something Gerard Manley Hopkins and the later T. S. Eliot could make valuable use of—which Kinnell could not avail himself of even though, in Davie's opinion, he has unrealized religious aspirations. To Davie, Kinnell deprives himself of access to the Christian tradition, to the powerful mysteries of the Christian Incarnation; he can merely suggest his unrealized religious aspirations by "tossing the name of Jesus around." More important, he loses a significant element that could make his poetry more powerfully dramatic by a lack of affinity for the traditional treatments of death by Milton or Tennyson. His poems can only convey the impression of being death-obsessed without relief.

Two poems in Kinnell's first book that seem to negate Christianity are "First Communion" and "Easter," neither included later in *Selected Poems*. In "First Communion" it is the boy's perception of Jesus and the Communion:

> Jesus, it is a disappointing shed
> Where they hang your picture
> And drink juice, and conjure
> Your person into inferior bread— (*WKW,* 5)

The boy here rejects the supernatural or transcendent element in the communion ritual, even though he otherwise exhibits great sensitivity to the natural beauty of the autumn landscape. He has likewise been responsive to the comfort of human love, represented by Uncle Abraham and his lover, "Asleep in each other's arms in the hay barn." Ultimately his vision embraces mutability, appreciating the change of seasons, as autumn approaches, as a stage in the process of the movement of all things in the natural world towards death. In the poem "Easter," Christ is avowed as a scapegoat who died for us rather than as an exemplar of the promise of eternal life. He is, in Ralph J. Mills's wording, "symbolic of the ubiquitous pain, victimization, and death of man and all other living things" (Mills, 143). The judgment made is that no religious assurance of eternal life is adequate to compensate for the terrible dying suffered by all things that live in the natural world. It is also projected that "God wills the suffering of individuals out of the paradox of a divine love whose goal is their purification and salvation" (Mills, 148).

The Self and Death

Ralph J. Mills is also sound in recognizing *What a Kingdom It Was* as a book characteristic of the sixties. It differs from Kinnell's earlier work in that he introduces his own angle of vision. He is concerned both with the necessary loss of that innocence which leads to the mistaken belief that humankind have any special dispensation from death and destruction, and the consequent gain of a "feeling of strangeness and then of terrible kinship" with all creatures subject to the same natural forces. The book looks to the sixties in that it is personal and radically concerned with the physical actuality of things, including how to endure the nightmare visions of reality.

In a recent *National Geographic* there was a cosmic-size account of the 12 destructions of nearly all life on this planet as recorded in the 800-million-year fossil history accessible to geologists.[6] Some scientists believe that all of these catastrophes were from the cosmic intervention of meteorites striking the earth or asteroids passing too close. This is the kind of cosmic inevitability that Kinnell appreciates. On the cosmic scale Galway Kinnell has his "own apocalyptic image of darkness enveloping a frozen earth," as David Perkins has aptly described it (Perkins, 575). Usually, though, Kinnell keeps his scale down to what one speaker who sees for all living creatures can observe, emphasizing this destruction in nature when most writers were stressing human-conceived destruction in a nuclear age. Kinnell's vision is personal, an effective small-scale version of this terrible destructive power of the natural world.

Man's own destructiveness is not excluded. "Easter" also narrates the morning news report of the rape and drowning of a virgin nurse. The rituals of the Easter service are no compensation for the murder itself since the ceremonies of the church are too abstract for the grisly concrete realities of earthly life. The service is characterized as remote, emotionless, toneless. The persona's realization is that not only are the raped nurse and the scapegoat Christ the victims of death, but so will be all the living: "We are dying on the hard wood of the pews" (*WKW,* 20). Kinnell particularizes this jurisdiction of death to include the child beside him comforting her doll. Finally, he focuses on himself, proposes his own death, and identifies with the dead "Virgin lady." Kinnell has exposed his involvement in death by contrasting the event to the abstract and irrelevant church service. He finds in all this no redemption for the raped nurse and ends the poem with her corpse moving downriver, a journey he empathetically follows. The poem concludes with a resigned acceptance that "It is as you thought. The living burn. / In the floating days may you discover grace" (*WKW,* 21).

Donald Davie perceives Kinnell as a poet who has religious aspirations but who cannot accept doctrine. Whether Kinnell accepts the doctrine or not, the word *grace* as used here is not unimportant. He seeks grace and finds it in death, in the eventual destruction or "burning" of the living and through the grace that comes from accepting and loving "the burning earth." This acceptance is not, however, without opposition, for it is human nature to resist. The important thing is not to shrink from accepting reality by turning to an escape through illusion. It is not by accident that some of Kinnell's best and most controlled poetry occurs when he is at his most unrelenting in his acceptance of harsh reality. If there is power in the poetry, this is the source of the power. If the forms become looser in his later poetry, it is because he finds free verse more congruous with the message that his medium must deliver.

The Propitiatory Act

Christ puts in an appearance again in the title of a minor poem and returns as the subject of a major one, "The Supper after the Last," one of a quartet of major undertakings in this volume. The minor poem is "To Christ our Lord." The title suggests a traditional religious poem, but the issue is more pertinent to "the one life theme" of Coleridge's "The Rime of the Ancient Mariner" than it is to the topic of Christ on the Lord's day. Like Coleridge, Kinnell is concerned with the propitiatory act, with seeking forgiveness for a transgression against natural life. It is a Christmas poem, the scene a family preparing for Christmas on a severe winter day. A boy sees the bird he shot being prepared for Christmas dinner, and he wonders why he killed it. "He had not wanted to shoot," but shoot he did (*WKW,* 6). He comprehends that there is nothing he can do but surrender to the natural acts of killing and eating the bird. He eats it as he killed it, with wonder for a bird "for whom love had stirred." This is a supper after the last supper observed in remembrance that Christ died for us. The commemoration here is for the natural act of one creature killing and living off another.

"First Song" treats a boy's initiation into happiness through accepting what is inevitable and natural. A small boy is "Weary to crying" and apprehensive because "Dark was growing tall" (*WKW*, 3). He hears what seems to be an expression of joy in the song of the pond frogs. Two boys bearing cornstalk violins happen along, and the three boys join the frogs in making music. The song thus created awakens his heart to an acceptance of the correspondences between darkness and sadness and this joy. The poem discloses that we have a recurring motive that becomes more and more important, not human defiance of death and dissolution but an attempt at finding compensation.

"Westport" is a landscape poem depicting a journey into the grass and forest country that had been observed by the speaker and a boy from a hill as they looked towards the prairies beyond. A dialogue follows: the boy's realization that "it will be a hard journey" (*WKW,* 12) is restated by the man, who adds "the hardness is the thing you thank." It is this recognition and resolve that make the denouement possible: "So out of the forest we sailed onto plains, / And from the dark afternoon came a bright evening" (*WKW,* 13). But the acceptance is complex, for the events of this evening lead to the shadows of night and to sounds of "the cries of the prairies" and the moans of the wind.

Kinnell can profit from observations of individuals as well as from nature, but much less frequently. He does disclose the perceptible loneliness of the poet. The poem "For William Carlos Williams" recounts Williams's reading before professors and "other lovers of literature," who grant the poet their almost total inattention. Williams is morally above declaring to them, "we were not your friends." He only smiles and endures "a lonely evening" (*WKW*, 22). He is insincerely congratulated by the chairman, given faint praise by a professor in tweeds, and none at all by another connoisseur of literature with a bow tie, who "scrammed." In contrast with this hypocrisy and insensitivity Kinnell perceives Williams's honesty in what he said as the equivalent of building for himself a "tower," a symbol intended both to praise the poet for creating something superior to his audience but also to hint at the poet's remoteness from his audience. The English critic Christopher Ricks judges this a failed poem because "its humor curdles to sarcasm."[7] This is certainly accurate as to the treatment of Kinnell's account of the professors in the audience, but the poem preserves a kind of ambivalence towards a poet he truly admired and yet regarded as failing to empathize through entering into the very things he declared to be so necessary to poetry.

The Major Poems

There are at least four memorable and even extraordinary poems in *What a Kingdom It Was,* "The Schoolhouse," "Freedom, New Hampshire," "The Supper After the Last," and "The Avenue Bearing the Initial of Christ into the New World." "The Schoolhouse" begs comparison with Yeats's "Among School Children," one of Kinnell's favorite poems by a poet who was his original exemplar. Assuredly, the design of the two poems is similar: a visitation to the school room, followed by some thoughts on modern education, a recollection of details and memories of the visit, and finally, knowledge gained from the visit. Nevertheless, the two poems are different. Yeats is the idealist and the Platonist; Kinnell is the realist and the naturalist. Yeats's poem is a recognized masterpiece of modern poetry in English; Kinnell's is only a slightly underappreciated, very fine poem. Kinnell's best lines come from his close focus on details like the benches and the broken door hanging from one hinge. He conveys a sense of the destructiveness of time on objects he observes rather than its effects on the poet himself. His poem becomes a statement of later dissatisfaction with the knowledge which seemed so complete then.

Recollected is the old schoolmaster, a "man of letters," who enjoyed walking in his garden, now occupied by "local tramps." Having returned to the house of the dead, the former student understands what he did learn then, the knowledge of death. Like Yeats, Kinnell finds modern education vacuous:

> Soaking up civics and vacant events
> From innocents who sponge periodicals
> And squeeze that out again in chalky gray
> Across the blackboards of the modern day. (*WKW,* 46)

The adult can now grasp "the first inkling" of what the child learned from the schoolmaster:

> Something that put the notion in his brain
> The earth was coming to its beautifulest
> And would be just like paradise again
> The day he died from it. . . . (*WKW,* 47)

This wisdom imparted that death must be accepted in all things makes possible an appreciation of the beauty of this world. The knowledge his teacher conveyed and what the adult poet has learned are recorded:

> he waved us to the night—
>
> And we are here, under the starlight. I
> Remember he taught us the stars disperse
> In wild flight, though constellated to the eye.
> And now I can see the night in its course,
> The slow sky uncoiling in exploding forms,
> The stars that flee it riding free in its arms. (*WKW,* 47)

"Freedom, New Hampshire" is an elegy for Kinnell's brother, Derry, who in 1957 died in his early thirties. The poem is primarily derived from memories of one specific summer he and his brother lived on a New Hampshire farm. It was a summer of learning what the adult now understands as signifying the cycles of birth and death in nature. Death is represented by the memory of discovering a cow's skull, but there is also a contrasting greenery on its grave; life is depicted by the memory of the birth of a calf. The two brothers enjoy the pleasures of summer, but they have also learned to anticipate its passing. Through their games they even become agents of destruction, crushing the flies that they had used to feed baby meadowlarks. "Freedom, New Hampshire" begins as a poem of these summer memories, but it comes to a focus on three moments of one brother relating to nature—his eyeballs with the clouds in the sky, his fingernails "with the thin air," his blood with the surf. It is this relationship with the earth that brings Kinnell back to thoughts of mortality and eventually to the repressed memory of the death of his brother. The grass can "be green for a man" in the grave just as it can for the cow or for the larks resurrected by memories. Kinnell concludes that "only flesh dies" but then the only incarnation he will know is "in particular flesh" that becomes the dust that "crumbles and is swirled again." The only shape it had was the man. He concludes:

> That was this man. When he is dead the grass
> Heals what he suffered, but he remains dead,
> And the few who loved him know this until they die.
>
> *For my brother,* 1925–1957 (*WKW,* 61)

"The Supper After the Last" uses a less personal persona, and instead of establishing a narrative base it "develops around a highly suggestive grouping of images whose source is inward experience, memory, dream, or vision" (Davie, 143). The poem seems Yeatsian in that it conjures up a wild man; but Kinnell's wild man is a scapegoat Christ, who "has been robbed by His suffering and death of the illusions of His teaching, His promises at the Last Supper." There is nothing life-reviving about this last supper. Kinnell's Christ speaks realistically and bleakly to the "lech for transcendence" of his listeners. His is a message of life without transcendence and death without any compensating intensified sense of life. All hope becomes mirage:

> The witnesses back off; the scene begins to float in water;
> Far out in that mirage the Saviour sits whispering to the world,
> Becoming a mirage. The dog turns into a smear on the sand.
> The cat grows taller and taller as it flees into space. (*WKW,* 64)

Our saviour's promise is only that:

> You are the flesh; I am the resurrection, because I am the light.
> I cut to your measure the creeping piece of darkness
> That haunts you in the dirt. Step into light—
> I make you over. I breed the shape of your grave in the dirt. (*WKW,* 64)

An American Ghetto Poem

What a Kingdom It Was culminates with what remains Kinnell's best known poem, "The Avenue Bearing the Initial of Christ into the New World." It was this poem that James Dickey speculated might herald a new age of poetry (Dickey, 134–35). Seldon Rodman asserted: "I do not hesitate to call this the freshest, most exciting, and by far the most readable poem of a bleak decade."[8] John Logan called it "A remarkable 450-line poem hard to match in American literature, drawn from contemporary life around Avenue C in New York."[9] Certainly to reviewers this poem seemed a new poem of the sixties, perhaps *the* new poem.

"The Avenue Bearing the Initial of Christ into the New World" is a very long poem on a subject even Stephen Crane, who explored it in prose, did not attempt in poetry: immigrant life on New York's Lower

East Side. It is also partly on a subject of great postwar interest that only Jewish poets have written effectively on, ghetto life, and even then, not in Europe, but in America. Lee Zimmerman identifies it as Kinnell's most Whitmanesque poem in technique and in its attempt, also praised by Glauco Cambon, to "seize the throbbing and shrill variety of New York life."[10] It is unquestionably Whitmanesque in manner, in its sights and sounds of the city, and in its cataloguing of the variety of life there; but it is definitely not Whitmanesque in tone, offering a modern, much less harmonious vision. Critics have admired the poem for its use of specific detail. If this is Kinnell's most accomplished poem, as well as his most acclaimed, it is interesting to observe that his greatest success at this time in his career was usually with long poems, not with short lyrics.

There is a case against this poem, ably presented by Cary Nelson, who believes that Kinnell has not satisfactorily concerted his vision with the descriptions of decay he has catalogued. In short, the parts seem better than the whole.[11] The difficulty which some readers have had with this poem is even more succinctly stated by Paul Mariani. It is "a poem whose parts seem to be continually sliding through your fingers as you try to hold the whole of it in the cup of your hands."[12]

It is clear that Kinnell's modern vision requires a dual rejection of Whitman. First, he must reject Whitman's optimism about America, the dream of obtaining through progress any kind of meaningful mystical union. Second, he must reject Whitman's romantic and very resolute conviction of a "sacred and sane" and "easeful" death. The personal loss of a brother and the recent history of the loss of life in the Holocaust were two poignant reasons for Kinnell to repudiate the Whitmanesque romantic view. And this is not the only rejection he must make. Mariani sees the poem also as Kinnell's attempted but imperfect renunciation of his Christian background (Mariani, 193). The poem is perceptibly neither Christian in belief nor Whitmanesque in attitude but Kinnell's own meditation on the inevitability and finality of death. If Kinnell has Whitman in the distant background of his poem, Hart Crane is in the immediate foreground. The tugboats of Crane's "River" section of *The Bridge* are still present in this poem, as are the derelicts and bums of the twenties. To these destitutes Kinnell adds some winos and panhandlers from the fifties. If Whitman and Crane seek a feeling of unity in America, Kinnell records the opposite, separation and loneliness. His poetic line reflects this disharmony as he breaks up Whitman's long flowing line with interruptions and fragments.

Avenue C was once one of the largest Jewish communities in the United States. Now it is predominantly Spanish-speaking with a mixture of Jew, Arab, Christian, as was the Jerusalem that Kinnell visited in the mid fifties. The poem contains long lists of people with individual identities and separate fates:

> A dozen children troop after him, barbels flying,
> In skullcaps. They are Reuben, Simeon, Levi, Judah, Issachar,
> Zebulun, Benjamin, Dan, Naphtali, Gad, Asher.
> With the help of the Lord they will one day become
> Courtiers, thugs, rulers, rabbis, asses, adders, wrestlers,
> bakers, poets, cartpushers, infantrymen. (*WKW,* 68)

The "lech for transcendence" characteristic of the nineteenth-century American idealism which culminated in the poetry of Walt Whitman is not only rejected but effectively parodied through Kinnell's use of traffic lights, much as Fitzgerald ironically used the green light at the end of Daisy's dock to mock Gatsby's dream:

> You knew even the traffic lights were made by God,
> The red splashes growing dimmer the farther away
> You looked, and away up at 14th, a few green stars;
> And without sequence, and nearly all at once,
> The red lights blinked into green,
> And just before there was one complete Avenue of green,
> The little green stars in the distance blinked. (*WKW,* 82)

In its representation of death the poem is distinctly surrealistic.

Paul Mariani suggests the comparison of the medieval "Bosch-like images of grotesque death" and Kinnell's goatheads and doomed goats lined up in the markets of Damascus, or the closed fishmarket, "the fishes gone into flesh" or "Butterfishes' mouths still open, still trying to eat. . . ." (Mariani, 197–98). But there are also realistic reminders of the contemporary horror of the Holocaust, with a catalogue of "Dachau, Buchenwald, Auschwitz," and others, and the unfeeling letter of the Nazi camp commandant with the blanks to be filled in: "Your husband, ———, died in the Camp Hospital on ———" (*WKW,* 78). For solace he quotes three lines from François Villon's "Legacy," which he has translated in his volume of translations.

J'oïs la cloche de Sorbonne,
Qui tousjours à neuf heures sonne
Le Salut que l'Ange predit . . .

[I heard the bell of the Sorbonne
Which always tolls at nine o'clock
The salutation the Angel foretold . . .] (*WKW,* 80)

The speaker waits, awake in bed, anticipating the vision, listening to the "dead spirituals" of blacks who sing outside his window. But the only response he hears is the sound of garbage cans being emptied into a disposal truck. The entrance to the avenue contrasts with the promise of the lady of the Statue of Liberty standing beyond the entrance to the East River. The avenue is "A roadway of refuse from the teeming shores and ghettos . . . Where the drowned suffer a C-change, / And remain the common poor." Behind the power station of Fourteenth Street, the equivalent of the fourteenth stage of the cross Kinnell saw in Jerusalem, is "the held breath / Of light, as God is a held breath, withheld." There are two possible solutions to this problem suggested by poets—Rilke's "resurrection of the world within us" through saying the words for the things more intensely and Whitman's faith in the power of words to restore the things they describe. Through our response to words with which the poet names things, we can see the object as if for the first time. Kinnell's poem ends with the knowledge that the heart "beats without windows in its night"; lungs "Heave and collapse"; the brain "turns and rattles" but the words have the last say:

In the nighttime
Of the blood they are laughing and saying,
Our little lane, what a kingdom it was!

oi weih oi weih (*WKW,* 83)

Long and ambitious twentieth-century poems in the Whitmanesque tradition tend to be more successful in lyric parts than in epic totality. The current critical consensus that Hart Crane's *The Bridge* was successful in lyric passages, less successful overall, as was even Whitman's "Song of Myself," could also be applied to Kinnell's long but much shorter poem. It is greatly impressive in parts but fails to coalesce as a whole. Everything considered, *What a Kingdom It Was* clearly established, as Ralph J. Mills commented, "the ground for his future writing," and it was impressive ground. (Mills, 162). Ralph J. Mills has identified the Kinnell territory very thoroughly.

> Also apparent in these poems is Kinnell's preoccupation with the larger metaphysical themes previously in evidence and now increasingly at the forefront of his interests. Death, suffering, the will to elude the body's mortality, and the brute facts of the actual world: Kinnell's imagination turns these themes over and over, dwelling on the insoluble enigmas of life's significance or lack of it as these emerge in the process of his own living. (Mills, 197–98)

Kinnell had also revealed some limitations in his view of his poetic world whose boundaries he would have to explore further in his later poetry. Some reviewers expressed the view that Kinnell still had not learned that his best poems came from rural experience even though, to the contrary, the most acclaimed poem in this volume was clearly an urban poem. Finally, and perhaps most important of all, he had yet to display a distinctive voice, an aspect of the new personal nature of poetry that critics were now giving attention to. Robert Lowell's new poetic voice in *Life Studies* was fast becoming the new critical fashion.

Chapter Five
Flower Herding on Mount Monadnock

Time and the Inability to Experience Eternity

Galway Kinnell's next volume, *Flower Herding on Mount Monadnock,* was a second book by a poet who had already earned noteworthy recognition from the literary establishment for his first effort. This time there were reasonable expectations which may have been disappointed after the measured success of the first volume. It was, once more, a fairly slim book, with more short poems than in the previous collection and fewer long poems. It was divided into two parts of almost equal length: part one consisted of 14 poems, part two of 12 poems. Kinnell's own later reevaluation of the quality of the poems in this volume may be indicated by his picking only 8 of the 26 poems for his *Selected Poems,* "The River That Is East," "To a Child in Calcutta," "For Robert Frost," "Poem of Night," "Middle of the Way," "Ruins Under the Stars," "Spindrift," and the title poem, "Flower Herding on Mount Monadnock." *Flower Herding* is assuredly not a book with many of Kinnell's most memorable poems. But in the best poems there is further evidence of what he had learned he could do in the best poems in his previous volume, staying close to a specific experience, conveying to his reader not only a strong impression of presence, of being there, but also an expectation of being at a scene which becomes the source of the meditations that ensue.

Reviewers dutifully noted that the mountain named in the title was in New Hampshire and that "monad" was the philosopher Leibnitz's term for an elementary, individual thing that reflects in itself the whole universe. For a central metaphor Kinnell had adapted for his purposes the microscopic "world in a grain of sand" view used in poetry by William Blake, Emerson, and other American transcendentalists. Kinnell's world of monads is examined by a poet who professed that "half my life belongs to the wild darkness" and who with a subsequently untroubled eye can also see himself as belonging to that darkness.

In his first book Kinnell had fairly objectively dramatized objects from the physical world graphically; in his second book he seems determined to be more personal, more introspective, even determined to face the worst in himself. Since his persona is intended to stand for us as well, we, as his readers, are expected to be willing to recognize the worst in ourselves as well. Kinnell's introspective look is to be accomplished after establishing a context of specific places and making references to poets that have meant something to him. In part one Kinnell is surprisingly urban, wandering about such exotic urban places as Calcutta, cities in Japan, and New York City. In part two he returns to his more usual setting, New England rural life, closing the sequence with his Monadnock mountain poem.

Galway Kinnell suggests in *Walking Down the Stairs* that a reader might see Yves Bonnefoy, whose *On the Motion and Immobility of Douve* he had translated, as an influence on the poems in this collection.[1] This influence is discernible in the first poem, "The River That Is East," because here, as in the *Douve,* we are adrift on the river of time. Lee Zimmerman astutely finds the epigraph to *Douve* from Hegel expressive of what becomes one of the basic propositions of *Flower Herding*: "But the life of spirit is not frightened at death and does not keep itself pure of it. It endures death and maintains itself in it" (Zimmerman, 52). He equates this expression with Kinnell's echo of this theme in one of his prose essays, "there is another kind of glory in our lives which derives precisely from our inability to enter that paradise or to experience eternity" (*PPW,* 125). Zimmerman also mentions, and I stress, that a major influence on Kinnell and on most writers of his generation was the postwar existentialism of the fifties. Like the existentialists and like Emily Dickinson, at least in Kinnell's reading of her poems on death, he goes a step beyond Bonnefoy and comprehends the moment of death as one of increased life and heightened feeling. For Kinnell it must be a moment about which there is always a requisite ambivalence, since his poems characteristically illustrate his dictum that "death has two aspects—the extinction, which we fear, and the flowing away into the universe which we desire" (*WDS,* 23). This dual view precludes romantic acquiescence by introducing in his most dramatic poems a conflict between what we fear and what we desire. This is a conflict, iterated over and over again in Kinnell's poems, that is usually absent from poems by his friends and sometimes kindred poets, Robert Bly and James Wright, making his best poems more dramatically powerful than theirs.

Kinnell begins his new volume still under the sway of his powerful "Avenue C" poem with images of cityscapes, but he never quite rivals the previous ones here; and he soon returns to nature as his more common setting and more pertinent to his subject. He is attentive to representing the relentless flow of time and to communicating the intensity of feeling towards objects encountered as well as the pain that this flow makes unavoidable. Kinnell's cityscapes may owe something to Hart Crane. More explicitly, he parallels Theodore Roethke in his use of nature for his own spiritual autobiography, trying to realize both a "poetics of the physical world," and, as Roethke required for the new poet in "Open Letter," to "face up to a genuine mystery" in language that is "compelling and immediate." Kinnell's success may be judged by how well he lives up to Roethke's specification.

"The River That Is East" begins as closely attuned to Hart Crane as Kinnell ever becomes with the substitution of the Williamsburg Bridge for the Brooklyn Bridge: "Buoys begin clanging like churches / And peter out. Sunk to the gunwhales / In their shapes tugs push upstream" (*FH,* 3).

He concludes the first stanza with seagulls, veritable seagulls in a scene much less idyllic than Crane's:

> Through white-winged gulls which shriek
> And flap from the water and sideslip in
> Over the chaos of illusions, dangling
> Limp red hands, and screaming as they touch. (*FH,* 3)

The second section of the poem opens with the images of famous dreamers from American fiction lying on their deathbeds—Citizen Kane, Gatsby, Clyde Griffiths—and then centers on a boy fantasizing about a "sick-hearted heiress" in the stateroom of the passing ocean liner the *Ile de France.* Section three moves to the perspective of a man on the pier who has given up on his dreams and illusions but appreciates the beauty of the snowfall on the dirty water. His last wish is for a beautiful death, possibly exploding in the water as one of the sea gulls. The last section imparts the speaker's own view, unillusioned, certain only of the onflowing river, obscured in "the mist beneath us," even accepting the vulture as "a vague scummed thing." He concludes that we have no roots "but the shifts of our pain, / No flowering but our own strange lives." The river is a symbol of the journey of the "things we love" to extinction: 'Towards the radiance in which they go out?" He has a final perspective: this is only "the River that is East, known once / From a high window in Brooklyn" with all the debris the dreamers fail to see, "swinging home again" (*FH,* 5).

"Room of Return" is worth mentioning as an additional river vista poem, the river this time perceived from a room overlooking the Hudson River, and with the speaker as more perceptibly the poet himself. He sees oceanliners without engaging in the fantasies of the boy in the prior poem. The scene implies a naturalistic narrative. Inside the room the objects include "a naked light bulb," "coat hangers," "whiskey bottles." Outside, his view is limited to the "alleycat" who "sneaks up / To slop his saucer / Of fresh milk on the fire escape" to wash down a rat he has just eaten (*FH,* 19). The poem is patently solipsistic. The speaker cannot relate to anything outside his own room, even to the oceanliners he knows go by. Nothing in the scene sanctions any transcendence to a higher level of perception.

In a similar poem, "Under the Williamsburg Bridge," the speaker departs his room and "broke bread / At the riverbank." But a black gull kills "the ceremony of the dove." The speaker tactilely feels the gull's work as a bird of prey "Tearing for life at my bones." His only solace is that tomorrow on the bridge: "Up in some riveted cranny in the sky, / It is true, the great and wondrous sun will be shining / On an older spider wrapping a fly in spittle-strings" (*FH,* 21).

In another place, Calcutta, and at another time, the poet looks out on a corrupted Eastern city, where illusions are still impossible. In this poem, "Calcutta Visits," Gandhi is in his grave, and whores are on the street; a beggar touches his knees and pleads for a morsel. The poet, bereft of illusions, can only sit in his room in the Grand Hotel, "drinking himself blind, / While the fan prowls the ceiling as in a zoo" (*FH,* 11). A Bengali poet acknowledges that he too looks from his window and "has to transcend its pain anew." There is no comfort from pain for Kinnell in the teachings of the philosophy of the East, though.

In 'To a Child in Calcutta" the poet grasps a dark child in his arms. It is a momentary thing; he feels that the child is his conqueror and realizes that when the child reaches his age, he, this stranger father, will be dying in a strange land, "his own." What will remain as a more enduring record is only the photograph of this gesture and the confirmation of "the pain of a little flesh" (*FH,* 14). This is a moment of rare compassion for Kinnell, in one of his more engaging and less noticed poems. If this is not a book of memorable Kinnell poems, it is one with some fine lyrical passages by a poet who may have the same themes but is trying to approach them differently.

Perplexed Poems

"The Homecoming of Emma Lazarus" represents another departure for Kinnell, who has been accused of writing poems inhabited only by his own consciousness. It is a peopled poem expressing disillusionment with this poet's and philanthropist's earlier optimism about the promise for the poor in America symbolized by the Statue of Liberty. With the New World, stripped of its promise as the new Garden of Eden, Emma repudiates her previous poem as "her hand / Hangs over the edge as if she has just let something drop." She shrugs her shoulder as if 'To drive away birds," which the poet knows had not intended to alight anyway. The old vow fades, but the poet with his experience of the reality of pain seems to accept the "wounds of all" (*FH,* 8). Optimism in Kinnell's poetry is earned through the ordeal of facing pain.

There are two rather intriguing poems about fellow poets, one on a near contemporary, "For Denise Levertov"; the other, on the grand old poet, "For Robert Frost." Each poem views the poetry of the other poet from Kinnell's own perspective, focusing on a reality each of these poets disregards. Denise Levertov recites with great intensity poems on her own sustaining "objects of faith." But she fails to notice a bum who "stood outside on Bleecker / Looking in through the glass" at her as she utters the word *solitude.* If she had glanced up, he could have aroused "the helpless / Witness crying again in your breast" (*FH,* 20).

"For Robert Frost" offers Kinnell's view of the complexity of Frost from his own divergent perspective as a younger poet. It merits being as well-known as Robert Lowell's sonnet "Robert Frost," where Lowell simply contrasts the effectiveness of Frost's momentary stays on an audience who are strangers to him and his inability as father to help those closest to him, his daughter and his son. Kinnell's poem brings up a question that still puzzles Frost's biographers, why as great a poet as Frost was needed to create the public persona who "talked so much." To counter this public necessity, Kinnell invokes a public moment of courage which has become one of the powerful television images of the sixties, the faltering old poet who could not see in the blinding light of sun and snow well enough to read his manuscript on the occasion of Kennedy's inauguration but who then saved the day for himself and his fellow poets as Frost "drew forth / From your great faithful heart / The poem" (*FH,* 23). He admires Frost because more than many of his early readers realized he invoked the dark beyond "the farthest city light . . .The night too dark to know," the "last leaf," and the "whiteness" (*FH,* 24). But he does not countenance Frost's strategic retreat from metaphysical incertitude to more manageable threats nearer at hand merely because he has "promises to keep." Kinnell regards it as habitual of Frost to seal "the broken lips of darkness" with "the *mot juste*" (*FH,* 24).

To Kinnell, Frost was "cursed" by not being able to commit himself either to "the mystical all-lovingness" of Walt Whitman or to "Melville's anguish to know and to suffer." Frost was not for Kinnell the terrifying poet he was for Lionel Trilling, because, though Frost made journeys into the dark, these were not personally terrifying enough: he was not yet "not fully convinced he was dying" (*FH,* 25). For Kinnell this is a truth that it is imperative for the poet to accept for himself so that he can then represent not just himself but even all other living creatures. For his conclusion Kinnell makes effective poetry out of the dramatic image of a poet struggling to maintain his personal order in a sea of snow. The image succeeds rather well.

Primitivism

In the poems comprising part two of *Flower Herding on Mount Monadnock,* Kinnell's primitivism becomes vividly evident as he invades the world of nature and faces wilderness, wildness, and death without signaling a Frostian strategic retreat. More than Frost ever managed, Kinnell writes with the authority of one who has had the actual experience of living out in the Vermont woods, being solitary, and yet coming to terms with his own loneliness. It is this accommodation that allows him to explore the contingencies of facing his own mortality. It is his intense concentration on the constant impingement of objects other than human on his life that makes it possible for him to perceive the object as monad, to accept it as a symbol for the naturalistic universe realized at a specific place and at a particular moment of time.

In "On Hardscrabble Mountain" the speaker stretches out on the mountain landscape and is able to see almost literally forever, "about a hundred miles," from the perspective on the mountain. He awakes, having lost the sun, and "shivering in thick blue shadows." He feels that the sap "had stuck me to the spruce boughs . . ." (*FH,* 34). He listens to the wind start to rise. He begins to pray to the animals that are beginning to hibernate, to "a bear just shutting his eyes," and 'To a skunk dozing off . . ." His prayer can be taken as indicative both of his participation in the process of losing his own individual consciousness and of an appeal for salvation, a more complex dual human response distinct from the passive acceptance of the animals.

In "On Frozen Fields," the poet and his companion "walk across the snow," under the faint stars, observing the moon "eating itself out," and "meteors flaring to death on earth" (*FH,* 36). The northern lights are seen as both blooming and "tearing themselves apart all night." They accept a role as a part of this cosmic scene, and "We walk arm in arm, and we are happy." But his sense of participation in such a vast process is momentary, like the very process itself—only "great an instant."

The solitariness dramatized in this group of poems is transcended only in "Poems of Night." In this poem Kinnell comes to see the woman as actually a presence whose individual parts—"Slopes, falls, lumps of sight," "Lashes," "Lips"—he acknowledges in the act of embracing and then perceives as basic to his own nature the necessity of recognizing something that at last transcends the isolated self. "You lie here now in your physicalness, / This beautiful degree of reality" (*FH,* 40–41).

This experience becomes something even more intense through his awareness that it is transitory as "the day, raft that breaks up, comes on." He concludes:

> I think of a few bones
> Floating on a river at night,
> The starlight blowing in place on the water,
> The river leaning like a wave toward the emptiness. (*FH,* 41)

Another poem, "Middle of the Way," designates Kinnell's obligation to Thoreau. It is part poem and part day-journal of a camping experience. He sees an analogy between himself lying on the earth, and the flames as they "lie in the woodpile." He is burning like everything else and represents an "imprint, in sperm, of what is to be." He expresses his distinctive ambivalence towards earth: "I love the earth, and always / In its darknesses I am a stranger" (*FH,* 44). The experience he relates is his joy of being among the elements even when he loses the trail in the snow.

The poem is concerned with his dual day-night lives in the wilderness: the life of loving the day in the woods, and that other life which "belongs to the wild darkness." The day experience is declared in the journal prose; the night experience is acclaimed in the poetry. It is this poem that concludes with two of the most aptly quoted lines to describe the poetic preoccupation of Galway Kinnell: "But I know I live half alive in the world, / I know half my life belongs to the wild darkness" (*FH,* 46).

No one has ever commented on "Ruins Under the Stars," which may prove that a sign of a good poet is the possibility of discovery of good poems that have not yet been admitted to the critically approved canon. This nature poem contrasts the ruins of what man has built with the continuing patterns of nature. What Kinnell feels in his loneliness in such scenes is a "homesickness" for something that he cannot quite identify.

> Every night under these thousand lights
> An owl dies, or a snake sloughs its skin,
> A man in a dark pasture
> Feels a homesickness he does not understand. (*FH,* 47; revised in *SP,* 57)

In this mood he witnesses a flight of geese described in one of Kinnell's most photographic descriptive passages.

> Sometimes I see them,
> The south-going Canada geese,
> At evening, coming down
> In pink light, over the pond, in great
> Loose, always-dissolving V's—
> I go out into the field and listen
> To the cold, lonely yelping
> Of their tranced bodies in the sky. (*FH,* 48; revised in *SP*, 57)

The word *tranced* is worthy of being explicitly designated as poetically felicitous.

Kinnell has asserted his admiration for Emily Dickinson's poetry, particularly for her poems on death. "A Bird Comes Back" is his version of a Dickinson bird poem and his tribute to Emily's "hummingbird." Kinnell's bird stings the blossoms and "wings crackling . . . needles the flowers" (*FH,* 38). Where Kinnell's poem fails to rival hers is that Emily's delight and humor are missing. His experience is simply "odd"; it's not at all one of an entire bird in motion but only the "bust of a bird," only head and shoulders with "nothing in back of him / But New Hampshire fifty miles away and badly faded" (*FH,* 38).

This gathering of relatively short poems ends with two longer poems, "Spindrift" and the title poem, "Flower Herding on Mount Monadnock." Kinnell directs his attention from man's "lech for transcendence" as only illusion, to his satisfactions from participating in the perceivable and dying world of creatures. In the seven sections of "Spindrift" he describes moments on the beach, reflects on his memories, and explores the meaning of his reflections. He starts with the refuse cast up on the beach, "old / Horseshoe crabs, broken skates, / Sand dollars, sea horses" (*FH,* 51), the debris of the forces of the sea. He then turns from the stasis of objects deposited by the sea to the continuing motions of the sea, the "sea-mud still quivering," and "the soft, mystical shine the wind / Blows over the dunes as they creep." In section two of "Spindrift" he directs himself to make an offering, "Pluck sacred / Shells from the icy surf" and "Lift one to the sun," as "a sign you accept to go / All the way to the shrine of the dead" (*FH,* 51–52; *SP,* 59). The next dead object he uncovers is a "little bleached root," which is "Brittle, cold, practically weightless" and "If anything is dead, it is." But the root is also a reminder of consistency of form or shape in nature. His attention reverts to the sea in section four, reflecting that the wave's crash on the surf "is the most we know of time, / And it is our undermusic of eternity" (*FH,* 52). He turns next, like Robinson Crusoe, to his own footprints in the sand, which "Already begin vanishing." In the last section, he asks: "What does he really love, / That old man . . . ?" The revised and final version of the poem concludes with an acceptance of man's congruity with all the other things that have died:

> Nobody likes to die
> But an old man
> Can know
> A kind of gratefulness
> Towards time that kills him,
> Everything he loved was made of it. (*FH,* 54)

The original version ends with a possible positive emendation. Man becomes a skeleton like the scallop shell but "Shining with time": "In the end / What is he but the scallop shell / Shining with time like any pilgrim?"(*FH,* 54).

The book's title poem represents a journey from the sea up the mountain. The emphasis, as he journeys, is the close observation of nature. He is here actually looking for some kind of positive experience, one without nightmares, "Laughing ruefully at myself / For all I claim to have suffered" (*FH,* 55). The setting is nearly dawn, a pastoral scene, with the sound of the peabody bird heard in the still air. But pastoral is never very long Kinnell's medium. Even in this predawn scene he thinks of a flower that cannot be touched. He remembers a black sea gull off Cape Ferrat "Straining for the Dawn," and his thought of bird song turns him to reflection on elegies: "The Dead rise in our hearts, / On the brink of happiness we stop / Like somebody on a drunk starting to weep" (*FH,* 56). His mood has turned to images of change. As he kneels by a pool, he discerns bacteria on a moss beneath his own reflection. He remembers the story of his own birth, two weeks overdue, weighing in at eleven pounds, "big as a policeman / Blue-faced with narrow red eyes" (*FH,* 56–57). The stillness of nature is replaced by the wind blowing, and the water from "last night's rain / Comes splattering from the leaves" and a waterfall "Breaks into beads halfway down." The thought of death returns: "The birds fly off / But the hug of the earth wraps / With moss their graves and the giant boulders" (*FH,* 57–58).

This ending is one of Kinnell's most striking. He unearths a flower representative of the dual forces he characteristically finds in nature. Its blossoms "claim to float in the Empyrean," but he recognizes now that it too is "burning in the sunlight." Its "appeal to heaven breaks off." "The petals begin to fall, in self-forgiveness. / It is a flower. On this mountainside it is dying" (*FH,* 58).

Ralph J. Mills notes how in a considerable number of poems written about this time Kinnell stays close to the "lineaments of a specific experience," which he tries to seize "through a literal concreteness" or through "an oblique progression of images," (Mills, 167). There is indeed a new concreteness about some of these poems. Kinnell can still never escape long from the bleakness of his view of nature, from acknowledgement of the violence and destruction in nature, and of the transiency of all creatures. There can, however, be something positive in a kind of dialogue of opposing views—between the hope that isolated moments encourage and the acceptance that immersion in experience requires. Kinnell acquiesces to death; at the same time he seeks more life, in a desire for transcendence and in a final acceptance of the actualities of man's fate. In this book he has also taken his first small steps towards a more personal poetry. Individual poems are not quite successful overall, but the parts are often pretty impressive. To express the situation, using terms from John Crowe Ransom that Kinnell undoubtedly became familiar with during his student days at Princeton, one might say his poems may lack overall structure, but they can be enjoyed for their texture.

At this stage of his career (1964), in *Flower Herding on Mount Monadnock,* Kinnell can effectively set a scene, communicate to his reader a sense of the actuality of things, and structure the flow of his thoughts. But he also seems to have two problems. He clearly gives the impression of having trouble finding things outside himself for his poems to relate to. To some critics there is even a second, more serious problem: Kinnell has fashioned an effective persona, originated some remarkable images, created impressive landscapes; but the charge persists that he still fails to create a distinctive voice, something that Frost was absolute master of. One critic summed up his doubts too severely: "Verse can only live through 'voice' and Kinnell has none to offer."[2]

Chapter Six
Body Rags

"We Crave Only Reality"

Kinnell's next collection, *Body Rags,* published in 1968, has to be one of the most difficult books in contemporary poetry to paraphrase succinctly. There are 23 poems in all, and 17 of these are at least moderately long and divided into sections. Almost half, 11 of the poems in *Body Rags,* were to find their way into his *Selected Poems.* As is usual with Kinnell's poetry, the longer poems are the most interesting thematically and the most successful structurally as poems. Once more, Galway Kinnell seems to have had difficulty expressing himself adequately and significantly in short lyrics. One has the impression that more words are required to establish meaningful connections between parts of his shorter poems. Kinnell continued creating the sectioned poem as an organizing principle for his long poems in his next book *The Book of Nightmares.*

Charles Molesworth selects a poem not included, "Night in the Forest," as an example of a shorter poem that does not quite come off (Molesworth, 103). The poem has two sections; both are rather short, and impressive only for their imagery. A dialectic is implied, but it is not adequately communicated. In the first section a woman is sleeping next to the speaker; he notices a strand of hair flowing from her cocoonlike sleeping bag, "touching / the ground hesitantly, as if thinking / to take root." In section two he hears a mountain brook "somewhere blood winding / down its ancient labyrinths" and sees

> A few feet away
> charred stick-ends surround
> a bit of ashes, where burnt-out, vanished flames
> absently
> waver, absently leap. (*BR,* 19)

Undeniably, this volume contains two of Kinnell's most justly admired long poems—"The Porcupine" and "The Bear"—and also what is perhaps his best political poem, "Vapor Trail Reflected in the Frog Pond." Kinnell chooses these and adds eight more for his *Selected Poems*: "Another Night in the Ruins," "The Burn," "The Fly," "The Falls," "How Many Nights," "Last Songs," "The Correspondence School Instructor Says Goodbye to His Poetry Students," and "The Last River"—another favorite of his critics, one of his political poems, based in part on his experience as a civil rights worker in the South in 1963. It is this poem that contains the motif of "body rags" which Kinnell selects for his title:

> a man of noble face
> sits on the iron bunk, wiping
> a pile of knifeblades clean
> in the rags of his body. (*BR,* 46)

This image, with the variants that he plays on it, is Kinnell's version of the Yeatsian "aged man." His concern with "body rags" is similar to Yeats's turning, after the desertion of his "circus animals" and the bankruptcy of his previous images, to "the foul rag-and-bone shop of the heart."

Kinnell's regard in this, his third book of poetry, is still that of the first two, for finding some kind of meaningful survival from the destructive burning forces of life that lead to death. The titles of individual poems are suggestive of his stress in *Body Rags* on last things—on ruins, a jet bomber, last songs, falls, the last river, and especially on goodbyes. What endures among all these images of last things is the poet's insistence on willed survival, on lasting until the end. Kinnell expands upon his theme in this manner: "If we are willing to face the worst in ourselves, we also have to accept the risk I have mentioned that probing into one's own wretchedness one may just dig up more wretchedness" (*PPD,* 215). After so much redundancy on last things, Kinnell must begin to fabricate something more than human wretchedness before reaching poetic closure in his poems. In *Body Rags,* there is uncertainty about what Kinnell has realized beyond "more wretchedness." Lee Zimmerman even questions why at this moment in Kinnell's career a poet like Kinnell should continue to write "if one doesn't like what one turns up" (Zimmerman, 83). The same question concerns other critics, a perception that something more meaningful be communicated, that some sort of vision should justify the probing. *Body Rags* is not the book in which Kinnell arrives at that vision; nevertheless, he has written for it some of his best poems. What Kinnell seems to feel intensely about in this book is the realization that "the naked dirty reality" he deplored in the city life of earlier poems must now be extended to nature. In the best of his long poems his exploration of the meaning of this probing into reality becomes more intense, more terrifying, slightly distanced only by a more frequent use of the relative impersonality of the third-person point of view, a perspective inspired perhaps by the writing of his novel, *Black Light.*

The initial poem, "Another Night in the Ruins," begins with a description of the movements of "a last bird" and concludes with the rejection of the literary archetype customary for depicting miraculous resurrection, the rise of the phoenix from its own ashes.

> How many nights must it take
> one such as me to learn
> that we aren't, after all, made
> from that bird which flies out of its ashes,
> that for a man
> as he goes up in flames, his one work
> is
> to open himself, to *be*
> the flames? (*BR,* 4)

This poem is also a remembrance of the death of his brother Derry, whose face he remembers seeing a likeness of nine years before on a cloud viewed from a flight above the Atlantic. He remembers what his brother used to say:

> He used to tell me,
> "What good is the day?
> On some hill of despair
> the bonfire
> you kindle can light the great sky—
> though it's true, of course, to make it burn
> You have to throw yourself in . . ." (*BR,* 3)

Kinnell finds the family to be one of the most fertile subjects for his poetry, as do other poets of the sixties, among them Robert Lowell and James Dickey. "Another Night in the Ruins" concludes with the image of leaping into the flames and with the knowledge that it is only these flames—not the fabled bird—that rise from the fire. The ruins referred to in the title are an old house that Kinnell bought in Vermont; one night there, when it was too cold to sleep, he wrote "a number of disconnected fragments, some descriptive of the place, some imagined, some memories" (*WDS*, 34–35). The problem in explicating this poem is the usual one with various Kinnell poems: the organizational principle is almost entirely imagistic, beginning in this poem with images of the birds and ending with fire to affirm the inevitability of change. There is resistance to any easy conversion of poetry into prose.

"Vapor Trail Reflected in the Frog Pond" has been recognized as a parody of Walt Whitman's "I Hear America Singing." It is reminiscent of Whitman in style although it recants his song of joy: "And I hear, / coming over the hills, America singing, / her varied carols I hear:" (*BR*, 7).

Kinnell offers a telling account of how he came to write this poem from a triad of feelings: his response to the beauty of a moment in nature, his memories of the racial violence he had recently experienced in the South, and the sighting of the SAC bomber.

> One very beautiful day I was walking back up from the frog pond, naked, holding my clothes in one hand, my mail in the other. I could feel the sun sending its heat down on me and the heat radiating up from the earth. I felt come over me pure happiness. I felt totally alive and totally existing in my body. Then I looked up and saw the vapor trail of a Strategic Air Command bomber, a terrible defilement. I had recently come up from the South, a land then full of violence. Vermont had been for me a retreat from the rest of America; that day I felt its sanctuary was destroyed. (*WDS*, 2–3)

Certainly the SAC bomber whose vapor trail is reflected in the frog pond is a powerfully destructive product of modern industrial progress that Whitman could not have anticipated. Kinnell's Whitmanesque catalogue is very much out of the sixties; desegregation in the South, with the "crack of the deputies' rifles" as they practice their savage reaction to desegregation demonstrations, with the feel of the cattleprod used for crowd control; and war in Asia, with the soldier in Vietnam as "he poisons, burns, grinds, and stabs the rice of the world." The fate of human flesh in Vietnam is graphically described as the eyes of the victims of war "gaze up at the drifting sun that gives us our lives / seed dazzled over the footbattered blaze of the earth." Especially impressive about this poem is Kinnell's ability to transform not just the sights into those of the present but also Whitman's optimistic sounds into contemporary sounds of the militant sixties, cracks, groans, curses. Whitman's is a song of celebration; Kinnell's poem is one of execration.

"The Burn" begins with a different image, of the "burnt land" that Kinnell wandered across 12 years ago, "full of sorrow." Now he walks into the pillared dark of the forest of Douglas firs, which seem to have survived out of prehistory and sees "in the grain / of a burnt log opened by a riverfall, / the clear / swirls of creation . . ." He imagines the woman addressed as Charlotte having much the same experience walking through a field of poppies on a dirt road.

> . . . tiny
> flowers brightening about you,
> the skills of fire, of fanning
> the blossoms until they die,
> perfected; only the power to nurture
> and make whole, only love,
> impossible. The mouth of the river.
> On these beaches
> the sea throws itself down, in flames. (*BR,* 11–12)

Kinnell has again perceived the whole cycle from creation to flames as a monad constituting in itself the fate of all creations. In his poem "The Fly" he can even see truth revealed on the same small scale as Emily Dickinson did. Because of eventual, inevitable shared fate, he can say "our last goodbye" to a creature with which he shares the same fate, "the absolute last, / the naked dirty reality of him last." He also pays tribute in this poem to another Dickinson fascination, with bees, describing the bee which "stings and dies" but brings life to everything "she ever touches" (*BR,* 14).

Howard Nelson has described these shorter and simpler poems by Kinnell as almost "runic," comparable to the Germanic riddle poems. Whatever flames or falls in nature, as evident in "The Falls," reminds Kinnell that he is subject in the same way to time and mortality. But it is not death alone that he experiences but also the excitement from the consciousness of death, of a return to a preconscious or animal state which permits him, after the terror of a dark night of the soul, to move back into life, emerging as in "How Many Nights" to hear a wild crow crying "'yaw yaw yaw' / from a branch nothing cried from ever in my life" (*BR,*

22). This poem is one of the supposed exceptions to the need for longer poems. It is an effective day-night imagery poem which sees God, or the "Creator Spirit" as "Maker of night and day," which walks out "the next morning over the frozen world."

Kinnell has described the tone of such poems in terms of the necessity of taking "seriously Thoreau's dictum, 'Be it life or death, we crave only reality.'" He believes that this is the truth that will set one free, and this truth requires an awareness of an intimacy shared with the subhuman world of animal life.

"Last Songs" reminds me not of Emily Dickinson but more of Robert Frost in its regard for the elegies of birds. It is a poem concerned with how to take "Silence. Ashes / in the grate" and to "reinvent it on earth / as song" (*BR,* 23). This is the question in many of Kinnell's poems, how can a person, particularly how does a poet, respond to silence? Often the answer is something either not there or simply not communicated to the reader. Lee Zimmerman draws on Barbara Herrnstein Smith's expertise on closure in poetry to describe Kinnell's endings as frequently "anti-closure, maintaining the integrity of the poem while avoiding a strong closure that might convey certitude" (Zimmerman, 102). The question remains as to whether this makes for good or bad poetry. New critical formalism tended to value poetry by the difficulty of the oppositions it was able to reconcile. Postmodernist aesthetics, poststructural criticism, characteristically, is more receptive to contrarieties and even deconstruction.

"The Correspondence School Instructor Says Goodbye to His Poetry Students" is a bit different from the usual Kinnell poem because it contains some rather charming vignettes of the eccentricities of other people and comes as close to humor as the markedly nonhumorous Kinnell ever manages. It makes one wish for more poems in this vein. The poem begins as a defense of his treatment of his students' attempts to realize their "God-given impulses / to write" (*BR,* 25). It ends with a goodbye to those "who are, for me, the postmarks again / of shattered towns" and who in their poems have given him their "loneliness" while keeping their "solitude" (*BR,* 26). He describes his experience in *Walking Down the Stairs.*

In the late fifties I taught a correspondence school course for the University of Chicago for a couple of years. There was loneliness! The people who took the course in isolation wards, so to speak, little towns across the country, where they had nobody to whom they could show their poems. I felt very useful, teaching the course, but it was very painful as well to be the one listening. (*WDS,* 11)

"The Correspondence School Instructor" is also about how Kinnell could, if he chose, write lighter poems that could still express human loneliness and solitude. It is possible for him to be lighter in tone in this poem because his subject is exclusively loneliness, not the deeper existential angst of solitude: "their loneliness / away in poems, only their solitude kept."

The Political Poem

"The Last River" is another one of Kinnell's successful long poems, characteristically divided into sections; and it is also one of his most directly personal since it is based on his experience in a Southern jail as a result of his civil rights activities.

Rumble of trailertrucks
on Louisiana 1 . . . I think
of the rides
back from the courthouse in Amite,
down the canyon between
faces smiling from the billboards,
the car filled
with black men who tried to register to vote . . . (*BR,* 33)

The poem is actually far more than personal narrative, structured more as an ambitious Whitmanesque exploration of America, the South, and the self. Kinnell's view of America is understandably more negative than Whitman's in as much as he recounts his Thoreau-like experience of being in jail, not just with fellow civil rights activists, but with the criminal element in contemporary America—a copbeater, a car thief, a pimp. The mood is more that of the Robert Lowell of *Life Studies* than of the celebratory posture of Walt Whitman in "Song of Myself." Kinnell's poem also becomes curiously symbolic, beginning as a description of the jail and then making the jail cell the equivalent of a brain cell through which pass memories of his trip South intermingled with early boyhood remembrances. The final section of the poem is political, issuing from the memories and dreams of an imprisoned civil-rights worker in the South.

"The Last River" begins archetypally with images of a ride on Charon's ferry towards Hades and then becomes quickly contemporary with the advent of highway trailer trucks and Southern police cars. Kinnell's Virgilian guide through this inferno is, appropriately, that other martyr, Henry David Thoreau, who engaged in civil disobedience and was also arrested in his protest of the war with Mexico. Thoreau is clearly more romantic, more transcendental than the 1960s Kinnell.

> Seeking love . . . love
> without human blood in it,
> that leaps above
> men and women, flesh and erections,
> which I thought I had found
> in a Massachusetts gravel bank one spring . . .
> seeking love . . .
> failing to know I only loved
> my purity . . . (*BR,* 46)

It is exactly this idealism of the American romantic past that has been lost in the violent civil rights encounters in Alabama and Mississippi. The last message from Thoreau is "For Galway alone. / I send you my mortality." Every high-sounding political speech fails with the decay of mortal flesh.

> Here his voice falters, he drops
> to his knees, he is
> falling to pieces,
> no nose left,
> no hair,
> no teeth,
> limbs dangling from prayer-knots and rags,
>
> waiting by the grief-tree
> of the last river. (*BR,* 47)

Animal Fabliaux

If Kinnell's next book, *The Book of Nightmares,* is generally regarded as his best book of poetry overall, *Body Rags* is remembered as the book that contains two of his most often praised poems, his two animal poems,

"The Porcupine" and "The Bear." These are distinctive poems that only Galway Kinnell could write. His need to transcend his human ego to arrive at another more primitive state of consciousness is facilitated by his empathy for these two animals. Both animals have a primitive resilient strength that the poet feels the exigency to realize for himself. Various analogies are made credible, between the animal and the poet, and between the pain and the death suffered by the animals and his own apprehensions. A strength of Kinnell's poetry, singularly demonstrated in these two poems, is his facility in his descriptions to be both literal and at the same time symbolic and mythic.

"The Porcupine" has an expository, even a logical, order, providing an ironic explanation of seven ways in which porcupines resemble man in general and poets in particular. Kinnell begins with a description of the porcupine as

> Unimpressed—bored—
> by the whirl of stars, by *these*
> he's astonished, ultra–
> Rilkean angel!
>
> for whom the true
> portion of the sweetness of earth
> is one of those bottom-heavy, glittering, saccadic
> bits
> of salt water that splash down
> the haunted ravines of a human face. (*BR,* 57)

Kinnell has remarked on his Rilkean angel comparison: "I was thinking—as I seem to do often—of the Ninth Elegy, where Rilke tells how the angels are attracted by ordinary, earthly things" (*WDS,* 111). I am reminded that Rilkean angels are also a preoccupation of another poet influenced by Rilke, Randall Jarrell, at the peak of his fame when Kinnell was beginning to publish as a poet. Kinnell's more corporeal Rilkean angel, the porcupine, is a voracious animal, glutting itself on its physical experiences as the poet must on his personal experiences as well as on the reading he must also avail himself of to write his poetry. Poetry comes primarily from the inner depths and from pain and self-sacrifice. For that reason, the porcupine is seen symbolically as Saint Sebastian, his quills as the arrows:

In my time I have
crouched, quills erected,
Saint
Sebastian of the
sacred heart, and been
beat dead with a locust club
on the bare snout. (*BR,* 58)

Kinnell draws on an Avesta mythology as ancient as the time of Zoroaster, which he most likely learned during his Iranian Fulbright year during 1959–1960. Among the mysteries of Avestian fire worship, the porcupine was valued because its quills radiated from its body like the rays of the sun.

The Avesta
puts porcupine killers
into hell for nine generations, sentencing them
to gnaw out
each other's hearts for the
salts of desire. (*BR,* 58)

Kinnell may utilize animals as part of his natural setting, but he makes it clear that he has no desire to write a bestiary.

For me those animals had no specific symbolic correspondence. I thought of them as animals. Of course I wasn't making zoological portraits. "The Porcupine" tries to establish explicit connections between us and porcupines. In both "The Porcupine" and "The Bear" the one speaking actually becomes the animal. Whenever we identify with some thing or some animal, it at once begins to represent us or some aspect of us . . . (*WDS,* 56)

He is clearly concerned with the mystery that the creatures who live with us on this earth participate in that we have forgotten. He is convinced that "To touch this mystery requires, I think, love of the things and creatures that surround us: the capacity to go out to them so that they enter us, so that they are transformed within us, and so that our inner life finds expression through them" (*PPW,* 124). What Kinnell seems to seek in his poetry is what Coleridge reached in "The Rime of the Ancient Mariner," "the propitiatory mode"—a representation drawn from the primitive rituals of propitiation through which man identifies himself with the physical world of animals, plants, and even inanimate objects to entreat for forgiveness for some transgression. The usual transgression is the taking of the life of an animal, as in "The Rime of the Ancient Mariner." Kinnell evokes natural objects in order to come to terms with time and mortality. This is, he believes, a characteristic of American poetry: to evoke physical things, to give them actual presence in a poem (*WDS,* 52). Kinnell's absorption in the presence commanded by physical things most likely comes from his interest in Rilke, especially in that great poet's *Duino Elegies.* Rilke sees the poet as a vehicle of consciousness through writing in a medium which permits the visible world to enter the poet's own consciousness, to achieve fulfillment and to permit self-discovery. The conclusion of "The Porcupine" suggests the mystery of rebirth. He prowls in nature as a "blank / template of myself . . ."

> where
> burdock looses the arks of its seed
> and thistle holds up its lost bloom
> and rosebushes in the wind scrape their dead limbs
> for the forced-fire
> of roses. (*BR,* 59)

"The Bear" is deservedly Kinnell's most celebrated poem. It certainly demonstrates, for once and all, that he can write a successful narrative poem. Other poets, including Theodore Roethke and Delmore Schwartz, have identified with bears in poems, but neither so much as approaches what Kinnell accomplishes. The hypothesis offered by these poems is that the poet in spirit always desires something aesthetic, be it a poem, a song; but in his own person he is ponderous, awkward, heavy-bodied. To develop this contrariety Kinnell constructs a more substantial narrative base than is required for most of his poems. The result is fortunate. The setting, in both landscape and time of year—late winter—is feasible for such an archetypal encounter. The hunter's hunt for his bear is efficient and primitive, and is used by Eskimos: a coiled sharpened stick is planted in the huge animal's food. When it uncoils after the bear has eaten, the animal dies painfully and without any danger to the hunter. Kinnell expresses his hunter's first perception of the bear through his sense of smell. He scents "in late winter," the "chilly, enduring, odor of bear." The poem graphically delineates the hardships of the season, of the hunt and of the bear's death. The details are about as unpoetic as poetry can become:

> On the third day I began to starve,
> at nightfall I bend down as I knew I would
> at a turd sopped in blood,
> and hesitate, and pick it up,
> and thrust it in my mouth, and gnash it down,
> and rise
> and go on running. (*BR,* 61)

The details are excruciating. The hunter must drag himself forward with bear knives clutched in his fists as the dying bear hauls himself over the ground with his claws. He requires nourishment from his victim, living off the death he has generated. When the bear dies, he must, for a time, continue to live off him. He will

> . . . tear him down his whole length
> and open him and climb in
> and close him up after me, against the wind,
> and sleep. (*BR,* 61)

As he sleeps, he dreams of the death of the bear anew. He awakes and does the human thing. "I awaken I think." What he understands from "the human thing" is that nature is restored: "geese / come trailing again up the flyway." The dam-bear lies, licking to life her cubs. Having seen the effects of the blood of the bear and having gained insight into the ways of nature, he concludes:

> the rest of my days I spend
> wandering: wondering
> what, anyway,
> was that stick infusion, that rank flavor of blood, that
> poetry by which I lived? (*BR,* 63)

Andrew Taylor makes it clear that "The Bear" is not a poem about "killing the animal in oneself."[1] The meaning is just the opposite. The bear's body is inhabited by the poet through an act of regression, a return to his origins. The poem develops into an account of the death of the ego in the poet. His exclusively human identity is transformed. The speaker has confirmed that he too "belongs to the wild darkness," but he has also unearthed a new and regenerative vitality. "The rank flavor of blood" has led to the smell of spring, and the poet has undergone both an initiation into death and a renewal. Through the act of regression he has experienced renewal of life. Kinnell has thrown light on his own poem by declaring his attitude towards death which he intends to imply in his poetry:

> The death of the self I seek, in poetry and out of poetry, is not a drying up or withering. It is a death, yes, but a death out of which one might hope to be reborn more giving, more alive, more open, more related to the natural life. (*PPD,* 222)

"The Bear" is perceptibly an unpleasant poem, definitely not for the poetically squeamish, but it is also one of the most forcible accounts of the ritual of death and renewal. He imagines this experience:

> and now the breeze
> blows over me, blows off
> the hideous belches of ill-digested bear blood
> and rotted stomach
> and the ordinary, wretched odor of bear,
>
> blows across
> my sore, lolled tongue a song
> or screech, until I think I must rise up
> and dance. And I lie still. (*BR,* 62)

Charles Molesworth identifies another choice poem in *Body Rags,* the one plainly named "The Poem" (Molesworth, 105). It is aptly designated in that it is on one of the great romantic subjects, connections between poetry and nature, words and things.

> On a branch
> in the morning light, at the tip
> of an icicle, the letter C
> comes into being—trembles,
> to drop, or to cling? (*BR,* 28)

Body Rags is a book distinguished primarily because it includes Kinnell's two great animal poems. Neither James Dickey in this country nor

Ted Hughes in England, both specialists in animal poems, ever imagined anything quite like them. Kinnell also manages to compose some of the most impressive fire and darkness imagery in contemporary American poetry. These two poems are known for their subject matter, but they deserve more attention for the craftsmanship involved in their poetic architecture than critics have been willing to give. Commentators have also been preoccupied with thematics, with Kinnell's effective, often powerful use of a limited number of dark and transparently "death-obsessed" themes.

The question after this book was where could Kinnell go next; what could follow the successes of "The Porcupine" and "The Bear"? Charles Molesworth detects in the poems in this 1968 book an important advance in Kinnell's movement away from the fashionable irony of 1950s poetry in the modernist mode. He has turned away from just a "suspension of irony toward the immersion in empathy" (Molesworth, 108). Not only is this new attitude an important element in the new postmodern aesthetics, it is also a direction Kinnell needs to take in his poetry to avoid a tendency towards a restricting solipsism.

Chapter Seven
The Book of Nightmares

The American Rilke

Kinnell's next collection of poems, *The Book of Nightmares* (published three years after *Body Rags,* in 1971), records some departures from his previous practices. His preference for the long poem has now led him to construct a 10-section interconnected series of poems, building up what is in fact one long poem through shorter sections. *The Book of Nightmares* is modeled on Rilke's *Duino Elegies* more clearly than poems by other admirers of this great poet—W. H. Auden, James Merrill, Robert Lowell, or Randall Jarrell. *Nightmares* is vintage Kinnell; nevertheless, he has also managed to produce what are clearly the most Rilkean of contemporary American poems.

Another influence has been identified, second to Rilke in importance, but still an important exemplar, Theodore Roethke's visionary journey in his protracted *North American Sequence.* Cary Nelson has pointed out that, as in the visionary poems of Roethke, in Kinnell's long poem the self is everywhere in nature and the ideas seems to originate from the senses. He finds in Kinnell, as he does in Roethke's long poem, the use of flower and flowering imagery to help advance an "unfolding form" that implies both death and an ultimate consummation (Nelson, 190). Nelson quotes Kinnell in verification of the kind of poetry he was trying to write. It is a poetry in which "the poet seeks an inner liberation by going so deeply into himself—into the worst of himself as well as the best—that he suddenly finds he is everywhere" (*PPD,* 213). For the sixth section of the book Kinnell clearly takes his title, "The Dead Shall be Raised Incorruptible," from St. Paul's First Epistle to the Corinthians, but the idea developed here is closer to Norman O. Brown's concept of the "resurrected body"—which he defined in his influential book *Life Against Death* as a sort of rediscovery of the sensuality of the body that the infant enjoyed.[1]

Five of the best poems in *The Book of Nightmares* were chosen for *Selected Poems*—"Under the Maud Moon," "The Hen Flower," "The Dead Shall Be Raised Incorruptible," "Little Sleep's-Head Sprouting Hair in the

Moonlight," and "Lastness." The persona is still the same—the voice of the poet that comes in the progression of a long poem to represent all creatures. But there is a difference this time. In its inception and at the conclusion this series of poems is more personal, featuring Kinnell in his new role as father. *Nightmares* is appropriately dedicated to his daughter, Maud (born 1966), and to his son, Fergus (born 1968); and Kinnell is fittingly less solipsistic, now as much concerned with their fates as with his own destiny. This new subject is indicated immediately after the dedication in a quote from Rilke:

> But this, though: death,
> the whole of death—even before life's begun,
> to hold it all so gently, and be good:
> this is beyond description! (*BN,* dedicatory page)

A Father's Concern

In commenting on this book in *Walking Down the Stairs,* Kinnell discloses that "from one point of view, the book is nothing but an effort to face death and live with death" (*WDS,* 45). This is hardly news for readers of his previous poetry. His constant involvement with the reality of death, with the impermanence of all living things, had been communicated to his readers more vividly than how to live with the fact of death. But there is, significantly, another difference in this book, proceeding from his care as a parent for his children. The father's concern is in the present; their concern is in the future; and even more significant for them, as children, there is the consolation of an instinctive faith in life the adult has lost. Kinnell explains in *Walking Down the Stairs*:

> They live with death almost as animals do. This natural trust in life's rhythms, infantile as it is, provides the model for trust they may struggle to learn later on. *The Book of Nightmares* is my own effort to find the trust again. I invoke Maud and Fergus not merely to instruct them, but also to get help from them. (*WDS,* 45–46)

Still, such help from children for a self-conscious poet is acknowledged by degrees. More evident to his reviewers was Kinnell's familiar attitude towards death, described by M. L. Rosenthal adeptly: "Yearning implicit in the living flesh is the only shadow of hope in this interim dominion of death." But this time "yearning" is not all. Rosenthal also finds "natural symbols of affirmation with strong personal meaning—the wife's happy pregnancy, the birth of their children, and the couple's sexual harmony {which} come through with such tenderness and, sometimes, humor."[2] This is poetry written by a poet who is aware he must now accept his responsibilities as a family man. Consequently, from the rituals of childcare, there are moments of realization, epiphanies that transcend the lonely sensibility of the persona. Now possible is an actual fraternity with others—not just through love for his children, but a new relationship with his wife, with another woman, with a musician playing Bach. Empathy has led to substantive expressions of solicitude for others—his family, of course, but also for a man found dead in a hotel room, for animals, even for the seemingly insignificant death of a hen.

Kinnell's greatest solicitude is for the fate of his two children as he and they face "time's passing." He recounts in *Walking Down the Stairs*: "In the *Book of Nightmares* I seem to face time's passing as if for the first time. It is bound up now with the twin fears that parents of small children feel, the fear of losing the children and the fear of leaving them" (*WDS*, 42).

He sanctions personally felt sentiment but avoids the extreme of sentimentalization in several of these poems. There is, for example, the moment in "Little Sleep's-Head Sprouting Hair in the Moonlight" when he takes his daughter, Maud, out of her bed to comfort her following one of her nightmares, a poem skillfully saved from sentimentality. His usual preoccupation with mortality still broods here, as in his previous books; however, the concern is not for the poet or very generally for humanity, but for those he loves in his own family. Beyond the personal sentiments voiced by a father, Kinnell, aware of living in a nuclear age, raises the question of ultimate concern for parents in the 1960s, the decade of greatest fear of nuclear annihilation: why bring anyone into a world like this? The nightmares of Kinnell's title are acutely a consequence of living in a death-dealing world. The sequence of 10 poems, each with the symbolic number of 7 sections, unfolds as a journey into the state of the poet's consciousness, which is replete with matters worthy of ultimate concern.

Lee Zimmerman concedes the significant influence of Rilke on Kinnell's sequence of poems. He suggests as another possible influence T. S. Eliot's quasimystical meditations on time present and time past in the *Four Quartets* (Zimmerman, 139–40). But this influence may be indirect, more analogy than specific influence, an inheritance from the last great modernist poem, on just about every poet of Kinnell's generation. The persuasive influence is still Rilke. Kinnell comments:

In the Ninth Elegy, Rilke says, in effect, "Don't try to tell the angels about the glory of your feelings, or how splendid your soul is; they know all about that. Tell them something they'd be more interested in, something that you know better than they, tell them about the things of the world." So it came to me to write a poem called "The Things." Like the *Elegies* it would be a poem without a plot, yet with a close relationship among the parts, and development from beginning to end. I did write a draft of that entire poem one spring, while I was living in Seattle. I didn't like it and I threw it away, almost all of it. One of the surviving passages became "The Hen Flower." Then I started again. The poem has moved far from its original intention to be about things and now probably does try to tell the angels about the glory of my feelings! (*WDS*, 35–36)

The most distinctively Rilkean quality of Kinnell's *Nightmares* Zimmerman identifies through a discussion of a quote from Rilke in a communication with his own Polish translator:

Affirmation of life *and* affirmation of death reveal themselves as one. To concede the one without the other is, as is here experienced and celebrated, a restriction that finally excludes all infinity. Death is our revered, our unilluminated, side of life: we must try to achieve the greatest possible consciousness of our existence, which is at home in both of these unlimited provinces, which is inexhaustibly nourished out of both . . . (Zimmerman, 131–32)

The Element Beyond Our Reach

Zimmerman appends to Rilke's avowal of life and death as ultimately one, a pertinent statement from Kinnell's *Walking Down the Stairs*: "In the greatest moments of our lives, we grasp that there's an element beyond our reach, from which we came, and into which we will dissolve, which is the mother and father of all the life of the planet" (*WDS*, 97–98). He concludes that *Nightmares* is an effort to come to terms with exactly this "element" (Zimmerman, 197). He suggests that the "action" of the poems in this book is visually represented by an alchemical print Kinnell found for the front cover of *Nightmares,* depicting two young angels drawing the breath from a dying man. In writing these poems Kinnell surely had in mind the new sanction his concerns as a father provided. He also seems to have arrived at a belief that there is a more intimate relationship between children and that "element" beyond our reach into which we dissolve and from which we come than there is for the adult.

In his new concern for something transcendent in *Nightmares* Kinnell alludes to the Gospels and finds occasion for positive use of Christian imagery. He is especially drawn to medieval alchemy, possibly influenced by his reading of Carl Jung's psychology, in his own personal equivalent of the search as a poet for the philosopher's stone so eagerly sought by scientists. He even applies alchemical lore to his interpretation of the woodcut he reprinted for this book. Kinnell has commented specifically on the structure of his long, sectioned poem in an *Ohio Review* interview published in fall of 1972, particularizing the effect of the birth of his two children, Maud and Fergus, on these poems.[3] The most fundamental element of structure from this impact on the poet father is the obvious one: the sequence of poems begins with a poem on the birth of his daughter and concludes with a poem on the birth of his son. Structurally, between the two births, there is a symbolic journey through some pretty dismal country, making possible what is, without doubt, some of Kinnell's most effective landscape poetry, one of the most impressive aspects of the work.

The opening poem, "Under the Maud Moon," begins with a journey up a deserted mountain where Kinnell stops to prepare a fire by a "wet site / of old fires" (*BN,* 3). He imagines that tramps have preceded him in building a fire and that they stood there, "unhouseling themselves on cursed bread," as far as he can imagine from the purpose of the communion bread. As he cuts the dry shavings of wood for his fire, he thinks of it as also being prepared for the woman he has left behind:

> for her,
> whose face
> I held in my hands
> a few hours, whom I gave back
> only to keep holding the space where she was (*BN,* 3)

These are among Kinnell's most tender lines, appropriate to the importance now placed on his version of the nuclear family. Alone in a rain that tries to extinguish his fire, he remembers the songs he used to sing to his daughter as remedial for her nightmares. He thinks ahead, of the bear he believes lumbering ahead of him on the trail, busily eating flowers, his fur glistening in the rain. He reflects back to Maud, awakening in her crib, associating her with flowers he had thought of in his description of the flower-eating bear. He imagines Maud doing something rather remarkable, reaching into his mouth in order to take hold of his song as he sings.

> And she who is born,
> she who sings and cries,
> she who begins the passage, her hair
> sprouting out,
> her gums budding for her first spring on earth,
> the mist still clinging about
> her face, puts
> her hand
> into her father's mouth, to take hold of
> his song. (*BN,* 5)

In his imagination Kinnell travels further back in time to a vision of Maud in her mother's womb, active, "somersaulting alone in the oneness / under the hill, / under / the old, lonely belly button" (*BN,* 5). The stream of "omphalos blood" hums all around her. Kinnell has come to see the oneness we continue to desire as something that is "set in our infancy," a time of wholeness before we were later separated into mind and body. With the mind at that time still a function of our senses, "we felt a joyous connection with the things around us." His thoughts move from the womb to three later glimpses of Maud sequentially, at her birth, then as a baby, crying in her crib, and, finally, as an adult in the future when she will find herself orphaned and emptied "of all wind-singing, of light," with the cursed bread of the tramps on her tongue. He understands that at birth the umbilical tie to both the positive oneness and the negative darkness of the womb is forever severed. The poem concludes with Kinnell returned to the mountain, remembering the song he sang to Maud, having learned from his experiences in nature the lesson of "the long rustle of being and perishing." This song may reside in Maud's memory, reminding her that the original feeling of prenatal wholeness is still imaginable as recurring at death.

> And in the days
> when you find yourself orphaned,
> emptied
> of all wind-singing, of light,
> the pieces of cursed bread on your tongue,

may there come back to you
a voice,
spectral, calling you
sister!
from everything that dies. (*BN,* 8)

"Under the Maud Moon" is also a personal future message for his daughter, a postcard for the future. In *Walking Down the Stairs,* Kinnell adds:

Well, at the end of "Under the Maud Moon," what I *meant* to convey was the hope that when my daughter comes upon hard hours in her life—as everyone does, I don't imagine for her any special miseries—she will open this book for what help it may be. At least it will tell her how much her father loved her. (*WDS,* 90)

In the next poem, "The Hen Flower," Kinnell contemplates the killing of a hen and is reminded of how little distance there is between him and that same darkness:

Listen, Kinnell,
dumped alive
and dying into the old sway bed,
a layer of crushed feathers all there is
between you
and the long shaft of darkness shaped as you,
let go. (*BN,* 14–15)

He interprets the hen's throwing its head back on the chopping block as a willingness to die, and he wants to instruct himself in his own comparable willingness to die. He then explores two different views of death—death as finality, as extinction, as something of which "even these feathers freed from their wings forever / are afraid" (*BN,* 15), and death as promising the experience of mysteries such as resurrection. Kinnell details that "The Hen Flower" was "the first poem I finished of the sequence"; one he admits is neither "entirely rational" nor "entirely explicable." It simply expresses the "dread that is the poem's starting point. It addresses the protagonist before he begins the journey of the poem, instructing him to let go, to surrender to existence" (*WDS,* 46–47). The sequence may not be "entirely explicable," but there is a detectable development.

In the middle of his sequence of poems, in poems five and six, Galway Kinnell continues his meditation on death. The fifth poem, "In the Hotel of Lost Light," is a dark night of the soul rumination. The sixth poem, "The Dead Shall be Raised Incorruptible," divulges the hellish inferno of human depravity. The title is ironic; the flesh proves to be far from incorruptible. In both poems, the source of life, the womb of the belly, is pictured full with death too. Kinnell remains singularly a poet fascinated with the physical things of reality. It provides a saving grace of concreteness in the midst of meditation. In the first poem, there is a terrifying image of a drunk dying. He describes flesh turning violet; and, as the "omphalos blood starts up again, the puffed / belly button explodes, the carnal / nightmare soars back to the beginning" (*BN,* 37). In the second, his most graphic Vietnam poem, the belly of a dead soldier "opens like a poison nightflower" (*BN,* 44). Kinnell has identified the person in "The Dead Shall Be Raised Incorruptible" who speaks the *Waste Land* sentiments, "Lieutenant! This corpse will not stop burning!" (*BN,* 45), as a soldier in some war, but most surely Vietnam. The man with the broken neck is also a soldier, but he is based on Kinnell's experience with other casualties of the violent sixties—a remembrance of lynch victims in the American South. Once more, much of the structure of these poems is provided through very concrete images. What is different about "The Dead" is that Kinnell is trying to express his outrage over unnecessary death and destruction; consequently, he attempts to make the testimony more personal to convey his own outrage at the violent history of the sixties. Kinnell is not usually comfortable doing this; he has felt, for example, that James Dickey weakened his similar poem, "The Firebombing," by being too personal. But Kinnell has at least created some very powerful moments by being atypically personal.

In "The Hen Flower," there is effective use of the image of the northern lights, flashing and disappearing in the sky. The persona believes that he can "read the cosmos spelling itself, / the huge broken letters / shuddering across the black sky and vanishing" (*BN,* 13). In section 5, "The Hotel of Lost Light," there is a manmade, much less cosmic message from lights in the sky. "I saw the ferris wheel writing its huge, desolate zeroes in neon on the evening skies" (*BN,* 36).

In the previous poem, section 4, titled "Dear Stranger Extant in Memory by the Blue Juniata," Kinnell once more denies status to the church as a place where one might look for guidance on life's uncertain journey. The poet listens to the church's sacring-bell, rung during the Eucharist at the exact moment of elevation of the bread and the wine. He desires instruction but the "chime" turns out to be only "chyme," a mass of semidigested food (*BN,* 27). It fails to create the miracle of transubstantiation, the transformation into the sacred body and blood of Christ; it is only substance to be chewed and swallowed. In the rest of the poem Kinnell shows that even the natural landscape has lost its force. The Juniata, which flows through the Appalachians in Pennsylvania, is no longer blue or virginal. Kinnell has explained that the Virginia addressed in this poem is an actual woman, living near the Juniata River, with whom he has had a long correspondence. She is "a mystic, a seer," who "sees past the world and lives in the cosmos." Kinnell also clarifies a kind of private joke in the poem. There was an old review of Malcolm Cowley's book of poems, *The Blue Juniata,* which contended that the region Cowley was writing about "belongs to the past, no longer exists." Virginia "found it amusing to have her own sense of non-existence thus confirmed" (*WDS,* 109).

Nightmares and Song

Galway Kinnell now sees poetic creation as a means of resolving the nightmares of dreams for children and the nightmare of death for adults. In "Little Sleep's-Head Sprouting Hair in the Moonlight," Kinnell returns to Maud's nightmares and to his song to ameliorate them. The poem is involved with permanence and change. Maud clings to her father as if he could never die. But he imagines her in 2009 as old as her father is now. His advice to Maud would be a message advising her to live intensely by accepting the world with its signs of mortality and with the inevitability of change, to experience the world as physical—"*here is the world:* this mouth, this laughter, these temple bones" *(BN,* 52). The poet father can read in his daughter's eyes her mortality as well as his own:

I can see in your eyes

the hand that waved once
in my father's eyes, a tiny kite
wobbling far up in the twilight of his last look:

and the angel
of all mortal things lets go the string. (*BN,* 52)

Two later poems, section eight, "The Call Across the Valley of Not-Knowing," and section nine, "The Path Among the Stones," continue the symbolic journey. "The Path Among the Stones," even for Kinnell, is unrelenting in depicting loneliness on a journey which is inevitably towards emptiness. It is only with the return to the mountain and with the birth of his second child that any resolution is possible.

The tenth and last poem, titled "Lastness," marks a return to the mountain where the sequence began. Kinnell is concerned with whether oneness is possible in a world of mutability where things die. For the poet this is at last now conceivable. He needs only to determine the nature of the song required to acknowledge such a world. The fire he has made continues to burn, warming "everyone who might wander into its radiance" (*BN,* 71). The black bear intuitively understands that he is observed by "a death-creature." Kinnell recalls the birth of his child, Sancho Fergus, whose great shoulders caused the rest of him to get stuck in the womb after his head merged. With only his head out, with "the ninth-month's / blood splashing beneath him / on the floor," the child, he thought, almost smiled, "almost forgave it all in advance" (*BN,* 72). The poet walks towards the overhanging cliff and calls out to the stone. The stone calls back, but as he approaches this echoing cliffside, he senses a line beyond which the stone will no longer respond. He stands "between answer and nothing," wondering, "Is it true / the death is all there is, and the earth does not last?" (*BN,* 73).

In this culminating poem Kinnell devises something as close to a metaphysical conceit as he ever comes, a reference to the ambiguity of zero representing the end of diminishing positive numbers and the beginning of a series of negative numbers. Positive and negative views of life and death are described as "walking away side by side with the emptiness" (*BN,* 73). This denouement is different from his usual practice, more like a remembrance of Whitman at the conclusion of "When Lilacs Last in the Dooryard Bloom'd" than anything from Galway Kinnell. It does summon back memories of the role of song in overcoming the effect of Maud's nightmares, encouraging her attempt to reach into his mouth and take hold of his song. This time Kinnell designates a Bach concert, suggesting that he now sees poetry, like the effect of the music of Bach at a concert, as the resolution of individually felt pain. He regards his own poem as a "concert of one / divided among himself" (*BN,* 75). It represents the "earthward gesture / of the sky-diver," in free fall to earth, accepting the necessity of his motion.

> the worms
> on his back still spinning forth
> and already gnawing away
> the silks of his loves, who could have saved him,
> this free floating of one
> opening his arms into the attitude
> of flight, as he obeys the necessity and falls . . . (*BN,* 75)

"The Flea That Is Laughing"

Kinnell's final consolation discloses a dimension for which he has not been given adequate acknowledgment, a trace of humor, albeit a dark, gallows humor. The proper response to mortality is what poststructuralist critics would prize as a binary opposition. The poet advises Fergus in Lastness, "Don't cry!" but he also says, "Cry." The very last comment is the laugh, and the creature who laughs last is a flea: "On the body, when it is / laid out, see if you can find / the one flea that is laughing." (*BN,* 75; revised in *SP,* 120).

Kinnell has pointed out that he also meant to imply that the "fleas on the body of a happy person would be a bit happier than other fleas" (*WDS,* 28). No doubt this is another dash of commentator humor added to the discussion. It is, however, apparent that with this volume Kinnell has become a more positive poet than when he was preoccupied with change and death. This long sequence of poems asserts that parenthood—the living presence of his two children—has altered the sense of isolation and "emptiness" expressed in the nightmare vision of his earlier poems. It is this new element that brings into "the central core" of the sequence "a sort of light onto—well, I could say onto any subject whatever" (*WDS,* 25).

The Richness of Language

The new textural richness of Kinnell's language in *The Book of Nightmares* deserves praise. Several critics have taken note of the concreteness of the language and the new rich verbal tapestry of these poems. As is usual with Kinnell, his treatment of subjects is imagistic; the most significant development is the way he finds a means of expanding and changing his image patterns. Cary Nelson has enumerated Kinnell's reiterated subjects—death, emptiness, flowers, darkness, and light—and the recurring images to express these of blood, bone, and stone (Cary Nelson, 77–78). If notice of the rich image patterns is appropriate, the poems in *The Book of Nightmares* are also open to a poststructuralist critical approach, as Nelson infers when he finds a "pervasive binarism" in the language. The fires are both "kindling" and "dying." The poet is "alive" and yet "dying." Kinnell clearly longs to make these polarities coalesce through language, through his artistry, and principally through the regenerating power of words. Kinnell's ideas may be the product of the times. He may have again been particularly influenced by a popular writer current at this time, Norman O. Brown, who believed that language can redeem the physical by elevating it to consciousness (Brown, 108). But this new emphasis could also come from Kinnell's great exemplar, the German poet Rilke.

Lee Zimmerman is probably right when he concludes on this book: "Kinnell does not set out to put things right. His poem, rather, verbally, reenacts a vision out of which things might be put right" (Zimmerman, 191). This motive hardly marks a major change of direction from a dark and negative romanticism to an idealistic neo-Wordsworthian optimism. Nevertheless, for Kinnell's poetry, and for the rather significant distinctiveness of this book of poems, this is not an insignificant advance. Kinnell has also found two references that make his poems more socially meaningful. The first is political—to the war in Vietnam, which he indicts as Christian man's extermination of his brothers; the second is familial—his concern as a father for his children. In "Little Sleep's-Head Sprouting Hair in the Moonlight," he comes to see the poem also as an offering to his son Fergus as a means of dealing with the father's death.

M. L. Rosenthal sees it a bit differently: "*The Book of Nightmares* grapples mightily with its depressive view of reality and with essential issues of love, and it leaves us with something splendid: a true voice, a true song, memorably human" (Rosenthal, 77). I agree that this book is more "memorably human" than the previous volumes. This achievement represents an advance for Kinnell. More splendid than any new philosophical implications that have concerned Howard Nelson and Lee Zimmerman, however, is what Rosenthal and most reviewers also admired, the splendor of some of the poems as poems intending to express a voice trying to become more "memorably human."

Chapter Eight
Mortal Acts, Mortal Words

"Yes, I Want to Live Forever. I Am like Everyone."

Mortal Acts, Mortal Words, Kinnell's next volume of poetry, published in 1980, after six years, is perceptibly a more varied and less unified book than *The Book of Nightmares.* Instead of being designed as one poem with multisections, it is truly a book of individual poems with much more variety, as if intended to exhibit the poet's versatility. Although several reviewers were less impressed with this book than with the previous one, *Mortal Acts, Mortal Words* has the distinction of being the collection which at long last affirms that Kinnell can write shorter and more lyrical poems quite successfully. He had succeeded before but not consistently enough to satisfy his critics.

There is also evidence that Kinnell is attempting to strike out modestly in new directions from a poetry for which, according to some critics, he had gone to the same well too often. He had repeated the same themes, utilized the same imagery, earning for himself a reputation as the American Rilke—preoccupied, as that great poet had been, with utilizing the word *death* without being totally nonaffirmative. Kinnell has remarked of his previous book *Nightmares* that he had thought of it as "one in which I could say everything that I knew or felt" (*WDS,* 31). It was, consequently, several years before he could let that influence go.

In a 1989 interview Kinnell responded in detail about the problems he faced:

> It seemed that anything I experienced vividly could find a place in that poem; the poem seemed to be a world for me. So in that sense it was a hard poem to let go because I wanted to keep writing it all my life. But what happened after I published that book was that I had a terribly hard time earning a living. For about seven of those nine years, I was living an extremely difficult life, often teaching in two or three different universities in different cities simultaneously as

visiting poet at the pittance that they pay. I was driving through the night and trying to keep myself organized. When I was at home, there were my children who had missed me when I was going around, so I spent a lot of time with them. That combination of bad working conditions and children whom I adored took its toll on my writing. (*BWR,* 172)

By the time of his next book Kinnell may have decided that he could not quite let that poetic world go until he had done something perceptibly different. In *Nightmares* the presence of his children in several of the poems had made conceivable a reason for difference—a specific concern for them and a rationale for being more affirmative about life. Kinnell had arrived at something close to a modest version of Wordsworth's Platonic belief in preexistence, of children coming into this world "trailing clouds of glory." Having learned from them, Kinnell now acknowledged a greater appreciation of where we had come from and where we might return to.

For this and other reasons, Kinnell's new poems are modestly more celebratory in tone, with some minor epiphanies celebrating affirmative moments in his life. His previous imagery had been almost exclusively images of dark and of fire. By the last poem in *Nightmares,* "Lastness," Kinnell had seemingly arrived at the new perception that "Lastness / is brightness" (*BN,* 73). In his new book he shows a growing interest in both images of brightness and in the harmony of music, hinting at "a music of grace / that we hear, sometimes, playing to us / from the other side of happiness." This music allows us to live "as other animals do, / who live and die in the spirit / of the end," which he refers to now as "that backward-spreading / brightness" (*MAMW,* 59). The poem quoted is rather ironically titled "There Are Things I Tell to No One," considering that he is unmistakably saying something more personal than he ever revealed before. Kinnell still sees things complexly, even those things he is positive about, asserting, for example, that even "the supreme cry / of joy, the cry of orgasm, has a ghastliness about it" (*MAMW,* 60). But he also announces in this poem that he has a new vision which makes it possible for him to say some things that he could not say before: "In this spirit / and from this spirit, I have learned to speak / of these things, which once I brooded on in silence" (*MAMW,* 61).

It is this affirmative spirit that carries over into *Mortal Acts, Mortal Words.* Kinnell desires now to declare more assertively an affirmation of life, even confessing, "Yes, I want to live forever. / I am like everyone"

(*MAMW,* 61). He at last seems to believe in the possibility of some transcendence of the physical, even seeing fractions of life as holy. His complete statement on "the music of grace" is as follows:

> I say "God"; I believe,
> rather, in a music of grace
> that we hear, sometimes, playing to us
> from the other side of happiness.
> When we hear it, when it flows
> through our bodies, it lets us live
> these days lighted by their vanity
> worshipping—as the other animals do,
> who live and die in the spirit
> of the end—that backward-spreading
> brightness. (*MAMW,* 59)

Different Kinds Of Poems

The reaffirmation of life Kinnell has learned from involvement with his children requires becoming deeply familiar with the world to the extent of rejoining the physical world, grasping it, savoring it, much as the baby gets his original pleasure from physical things.

Mortal Acts, Mortal Words also marks an attempt to write different kinds of shorter poems, resulting in 41 lyrics in all. He thought well enough of his efforts to select a large number, 14, for his *Selected Poems,* including some of the most critically acclaimed—"Fergus Falling," "After Making Love We Hear Footsteps," "Saint Francis and the Sow," "Wait," "Daybreak," "The Gray Heron," "Blackberry Eating," "There Are Things I Tell to No One," "Goodbye," "Memory of Wilmington," "The Still Time," "The Apple Tree," "The Milk Bottle," and "Flying Home." Harold Bloom wrote the review in the *New York Times Book Review* and took this opportunity to pass judgment on 20 years of Kinnell's career as a poet. To Bloom, Kinnell was a poet of an emotional directness matched among his contemporaries only by James Wright and Philip Levine. He had the adeptness "to write with such emotional directness, without falling into mere pathos, the usual fate of American poets who speak straight forth out of the self."[1] Kinnell may avoid pathos, but he does not in Bloom's judgment avoid an "overambition" that leads him to try to make a crucial event out of each and every poem. To Bloom a poet must be at least a craftsman on the level of Hart Crane to achieve that kind of aspired intensity, and he discerns that Kinnell is no Crane. He can build up enormous tensions, but he cannot maintain them "gracefully," lacking both the necessary sense of design and the appropriate diction. Bloom selects for special praise three poems—"There Are Things I Tell to No One," "Wait," and "The Gray Heron." He also admires the descriptive power in "Flying Home," but these are the only poems he values in this volume. Overall, for this major critic, *Mortal Acts, Mortal Words* unmistakably represents a falling off in Kinnell's powers.

The poet-reviewer Hank Lazer confirmed that Kinnell tries to depart from his past works in this volume. He is attempting to write variously different kinds of poems, and he is also trying to substantiate that he is not entirely negative but at least capable of modest testaments of affirmation. Lazer believes that Kinnell succeeds through this wider range of poems in exhibiting that he is not a derivative poet even though he has traveled over the same terrain that Rilke staked out in "the life-death interface." His entry into Rilke territory is actually, in Lazer's view, "by his own vision . . . by his own lights."[2] Kinnell is obviously writing for the already converted in Lazer, who does not find Kinnell limited in themes or bleak and negative in attitude and who detects "throughout this book, happy, glorious, celebratory lines" from a poet who now clearly "takes a great and rich joy in this world" in spite of all the death and destruction he acknowledges (Lazer, 108). The "advance" that *Mortal Acts, Mortal Words* marks in Kinnell's poetry comes from his "greater certainty of those impermanent but perfect moments of celebration" (Lazer, 108).

I would agree that this is Kinnell's most Whitmanesque and hopeful book, but one should not expect emphatic disclosures on the scale of major epiphanies. Lazer overstates a positive message when he contends that Kinnell, like Whitman, is trying to show us that all life, including our own life, is holy; but it is clear that Kinnell is now moving beyond the Rilkean task of simply writing about death without negation and clearly deviating from his own preoccupation with the propitiatory act to proclaiming more obvious moderate celebrations of life. In "There Are Things I Tell to No One" Kinnell is unmistakably more positive about both life itself and the possibility of life after death: "I know now, the singing / of mortal lives, waves of spent existence / which flow toward, and toward, and on which we flow / and grow drowsy and become fearless again" (*MAMW,* 62).

It is apparent in *Mortal Acts, Mortal Words* that it is Kinnell's appreciation of the beauty of the world and his now mature understanding of love itself earned from his love of wife, of children, the new inclusion in his poetry of family, that produce the difference. He has arrived at the insight that when we become familiar with specific things in our world and accept both their perishability and the necessity of acknowledging that we too are bound to this physical world, at that time we can experience a kind of transcendence. His new "lech for transcendence" comes not from transcending the physical world but rather from seeking an intense union with it. Lazer quotes the most pertinent passages from Kinnell's essay on these matters, "Poetry, Personality, and Death" (1971):

> Don't we go sightseeing in cars, thinking we can experience a landscape by looking at it through a glass? A baby takes pleasure in seeing a thing, yes, but seeing is a first act. For fulfillment the baby must reach out, grasp it, put it in his mouth, suck it, savor it, taste it, manipulate it, smell it, physically be one with it. From here comes our notion of heaven itself. Every experience of happiness in later life is a stirring of that ineradicable memory of once belonging wholly to the life of the planet. (*PPD,* 217)

The Physical Things of This World

Kinnell does celebrate the physical things of this world more enthusiastically in this book than he has in previous books. The poet of the "life-death interface" has even composed a Franciscan poem, "Saint Francis and the Sow," contending, in imitation of Saint Francis, that the poet must "reteach a thing its loveliness," as he in effect does when he touches a bud.

> The bud
> stands for all things,
> even for those things that don't flower,
> for everything flowers, from within, of self-blessing;
> though sometimes it is necessary

to reteach a thing its loveliness,
to put a hand on its brow
of the flower
and retell it in words and in touch
it is lovely
until it flowers again from within, of self-blessing; (*MAMW,* 9)

The analogy is between the poet and the bud and Saint Francis and the sow when he "told her in words and in touch / . . . the long, perfect loveliness of sow" (*MAMW,* 9). Not only should this poem be taken as an example of a more positive celebration of the world but also it should be considered a contribution to Kinnell's bestiary of animal poems. It is, unfortunately, a poem often overlooked. It is the kind of poem that proves that Kinnell is more diverse than some critics have admitted.

The physical world may not always be quite as human beings expect it to be. In "The Gray Heron" when Kinnell seeks the hero that "stalked out of sight," he finds instead—what he refers to in his essay "Poetics of the Physical World"—"the return to the quiescence of the inorganic world" (*PPW,* 123). In attempting to pursue the heron he discovers instead

. . . a three-foot-long lizard
in ill-fitting skin
and with linear mouth
expressive of the even temper
of the mineral kingdom.
It stopped and tilted its head,
which was much like
a fieldstone with an eye
in it, which was watching me
to see if I would go
or change into something else. (*MAMW,* 20)

Kinnell can now articulate the surprises nature has in store for the poet in a fresh way, almost as playfully and yet seriously as Robert Frost could. But the old attitudes are hard to change. In "Goodbye," a poem describing the death of his mother, Kinnell concludes: "It is written in our hearts, the emptiness is all. / That is how we have learned, the embrace is all" (*MAMW,* 39). Apparently, when one is faced with the dissolution of human relationships, a last human gesture of love is imperative.

Lee Zimmerman finds less evolution in this volume than my reading discloses. To him it is simply a refashioning of: "Like Yeats his master, Kinnell spends his career working the same set of insights, but, predicated on changing experience, these are refashioned at every point" (Zimmerman, 103). The truth of the matter is that Kinnell now divulges more of a conflict between a realization of the truth of meaninglessness and the human need to persist in finding something meaningful. If *Mortal Acts, Mortal Words* is in some degree written about Kinnell's own changed situation, the poem "Wait" seems to declare his new attitude.

> Personal events will become interesting again.
> Hair will become interesting.
> Pain will become interesting.
> Buds that open out of season will become interesting.
> Second-hand gloves will become lovely again;
> their memories are what give them
> the need for other hands. And the desolation
> of lovers is the same: that enormous emptiness
> carved out of such tiny beings as we are
> asks to be filled; the need
> for the new love *is* faithfulness to the old. (*MAMW,* 15)

This poem seems also to contemplate the relatively long delay between this volume and his previous collection of poems. The reason, as suggested in the discussion in the previous chapter, was that Kinnell was convinced that the poem "Nightmares" in *The Book of Nightmares* was the "one in which I could say everything that I knew or felt." He goes on to comment: "I felt I could spend the rest of my life writing it—revising and perfecting it" (*WDS,* 31). He adds a significant remark on his concern with death. "The most difficult thing for the human being is the knowledge that he will die . . . we develop, one after another, some manner of accounting for death, or of turning it aside . . . of making it tolerable" (*WDS,* 97).

In "The Sadness of Brothers," Kinnell again confronts the death of his brother: "But this morning, I don't know why, / twenty-one years too late, / I imagine him back" (*MAMW,* 33). And he remembers his brother's desire to fly until the experience of actual pilot training in 1943, "when original fear / washed out / all the flyingness in him" (*MAMW,* 34). This is a neglected but rather striking poem in which Kinnell tallies the effect of this "original fear" on their father and on himself.

> In this brother
> I remember back, I see the father
> I had so often seen in him . . . and known
> in my own bones, too: (*MAMW,* 34)

In the last section Kinnell realizes the power of memory in retaining the acts of love and of the love itself that these memories keep alive. He answers his doubts about the effect of time: "But no, that's fear's reading . . ." It is not love, or acts of love like the "embrace in the doorway" but "only what the flesh can bear surrenders to time" (*MAMW,* 36). In *Walking Down the Stairs* Kinnell commented on his developing interest in finding his poems in the more normal affairs of human existence: "But whatever my poetry will be, from now on it will no doubt come out of this involvement in the ordinary" (*WDS,* 85). If there is a major change in his poetry, it is towards this kind of involvement. "The Sadness of Brothers" concludes with full awareness of his ability to find meaning in ordinary things:

> fat-gathering bodies, with sore, well or badly spent,
> but spent, hearts, we hold each other, friends to reality,
> knowing the ordinary sadness of brothers. (*MAMW,* 37)

"Wait" unquestionably deserves acknowledgement as one of Kinnell's most memorable lyrics. It advances one of the most conceivably lyrical of themes, how love and loss are inextricably bound together, another important recurring theme in Kinnell's poetry. For example, the poem "Little Sleep's-Head Sprouting Hair in the Moonlight" in his previous book concludes:

> Little sleep's-head sprouting hair in the moonlight,
> when I come back,
> we will go out together,
> we will walk out together among
> the ten thousand things,
> each scratched in time with such knowledge, *the wages*
> *of dying is love* (*BN,* 53; revised in *SP,* 115)

"Everyone Who Truly Sings Is Beautiful"

One of Galway Kinnell's messages, reiterated throughout his poems, is that the process of resolution always begins with the acknowledgment of a problem. In Kinnell's novel, *Black Light,* the old opium smoker Jamshid learns that he must dance on his own grave in order to renew himself. Renewal obviously requires more than mere acknowledgment of death. It also includes the outward process of empathetically entering into things of this world which are exterior to ourselves. To describe this kind of state, Kinnell invokes an analogy with the feelings invoked by music, specifically by song. In his early poem "First Song" Kinnell had described the farm boy who, on his cornstalk violin, was capable of producing a music which awakened him "to the darkness and into the sadness of joy" (*WKIW,* 3). In *Mortal Acts, Mortal Words* and in subsequent poems resolution of the fact of death requires the act of song.

> Everyone who truly sings is beautiful.
> Even sad music
> requires an absolute happiness:
> eyes, nostrils, mouth strain together in quintal harmony
> to sing Joy and Death well.
> "The Choir" (*MAMW,* 10)

In "Brother of My Heart," a poem of friendship dedicated to Etheridge Knight, Kinnell concludes:

> sing, even if you cry; the bravery
> of the crying turns it into the true song; soul brother
> in heaven, on earth
> broken heart brother, sing to us
> here, in this place that loses its brothers,
> in this emptiness only the singing sometimes almost fills. (*MAMW,* 12)

"In the Bamboo Hut" he recalls "the voices / of the washerwomen at the stream." The sound is remembered as

> . . . a sound like the aftersinging
> from those nights when we would sing and cry
> for one another our last breathing,
> under the sign of the salamander,

> who still clings, motionless, attentive,
> skeleton of desire inside the brain. (*MAMW,* 21)

In "The Still Time" Kinnell recollects his aspirations for which later he was to find song:

> . . . those summer nights
> when I was young and empty,
> when I lay through darkness
> wanting, wanting,
> knowing
> I would have nothing of anything I wanted—
> that total craving
> that hollows the heart out irreversibly. (*MAMW,* 57)

Later in life these old voices speak again:

> saying there is time, still time
> for those who can groan
> to sing,
> for those who can sing to heal themselves. (*MAMW,* 58)

The significant consolation provided by music, the reconciliation through song, is concisely stated in the final poem, "There Are Things I Tell to No One." And this time Kinnell is able to name where it comes from. The key passage quoted from "There Are Things I Tell to No One" becomes the key passage for the book. Once more:

> I say "God"; I believe,
> rather, in a music of grace
> that we hear, sometimes, playing to us
> from the other side of happiness. (*MAMW,* 59)

Involvement in The Ordinary: The Fergus Poems

Mortal Acts, Mortal Words opens with poems from what seems to be a growing family saga. John Unterecker uses an analogy with musical motifs to find the Fergus poems to be "opening notes" in the big musical context of the "large structure" of *Mortal Acts, Mortal Words.*[3] Not only is music important thematically to Kinnell; it has become important structurally. Unterecker designates part one of this poetry collection an initial brief *allegretto* that leads into "a sustained *allegro vivace,* the latter gradually shifting into *andante,* perhaps one marked *andante elegiaco.* Part two is a *scherzo.* Part three is *adagio lamentoso.* Part four is all *allegretto maestoso,* poetry recapitulating earlier materials but now enlarging them to generalization." The book furnishes the reader with "Mortal wages": songs that both accept mortality and celebrate our most meaningful experience—human love. Whether musical structure is perceptible or not, there is music in the poems, in the rich patterns of sound. The distance between Kinnell's meditations and the rich musicality of the great romantic ode is not great, and in *Mortal Acts* he has lessened that distance.

In "Fergus Falling" the affection Kinnell feels for his son is both personally meaningful and symbolically decisive as consolation for man's fate. The poem describes young Fergus climbing up to the top of the pine tree, looking down at "Bruce Pond," and culminates in his falling. The sound of the fall penetrates through the noise of the band saw his father is working, summoning the boy's parents to his fallen body. Icarus-like, Fergus has risked death; but his mood is triumphant. He announces: "I saw a pond" (*MAMW,* 4). The poem concludes with a father recognizing that what his son saw was worth the risk of death: "Yes—a pond that lets off its mist / on clear afternoons of August, in that valley / to which many have come, for their reasons." In his interpretation, Unterecker emphasizes the subtle music in this poem, noting its repetitions, rhymes, and partial rhymes, and the echo of all the "I's" in the poem. He is one of the few critics to stress the generally unrecognized artistry of Kinnell's poems.

Unterecker reclaims another poem for explication, a poem seemingly so slight as to escape notice: "After Making Love We Hear Footsteps" (Unterecker, 231). I mention it to illustrate that Kinnell is capable of a lighter touch. This is another personal poem that finds significant meaning in simple human gestures. The father recounts simply how his son can sleep through any noise his parents make except for their lovemaking. On such an occasion Fergus appears in his baseball pajamas and asks: "'Are you loving and snuggling? May I join?' / He flops down between us and hugs us and snuggles himself to sleep, / his face gleaming with satisfaction at being this very child" (*MAMW,* 5). The parents smile and fondle this "sleeper only the mortal sounds can sing awake, / this blessing love gives again into our arms." When he turns to his family, Kinnell can do very well with ordinary things.

The third Fergus poem, "Angling, A Day," is a narrative of father and son fishing all the best fishing holes in Vermont. This expedition is barren of fish, and the father fears that his son ". . . must be thoroughly / defeated, and his noble passion for fishing / perhaps broken . . ." (*MAMW,* 8). But Fergus accepts the failure philosophically: "'I'm disappointed,' he says 'but not discouraged. / I'm not saying I'm a fisherman, but fishermen know / there are days when you don't catch anything.'" The father realizes that for his son this has been a minor, but still important, "rite of passage."

I view with special favor the activity poem, "On the Tennis Court at Night." Galway Kinnell is a fairly avid tennis player, an avocation he shares with many other poets including Robert Frost, Ezra Pound, Hart Crane, John Berryman, Theodore Roethke, and Randall Jarrell. These poets talked about tennis but failed to write a good tennis poem. Kinnell has managed an almost mock epic description of absurd yet heroic human behavior in a tennis match begun in the moonlight and continued through a snowfall which manages to provide natural light against the contrasting blackness of the night and the darkness of the surrounding wood. The men continue their game not only against this darkness but as Kinnell realizes in a marvelous statement against "all the winters to come."

> . . . the snow blows down
> and swirls about our legs, darkness flows
> across a disappearing patch of green-painted asphalt
> in the north country, where four men,
> half-volleying, poaching, missing, grunting,
> begging mercy of their bones, hold their ground,
> as winter comes on, all the winters to come. (*MAMW,* 29)

This is a poem that clearly deserves attention.

In *Mortal Acts, Mortal Words,* there is now a definite and a significant attempt on Kinnell's part to make poetry out of both personal and more ordinary experiences—a failed fishing trip, a child joining his parents in bed, a night tennis match among friends. I believe that he does this successfully and that it is a needed and welcome development in his poetry.

Two of the short poems may be on more ordinary subjects for Galway Kinnell, but they are almost extraordinary as poems. "Daybreak" describes a movement, seemingly contrary to the title, of starfishes sinking into "the tidal mud, just before sunset." It states Kinnell's belief of being in contact with the earth. The paradox is that to ascend everything must descend. But descending into the psyche one does not necessarily lose touch with the stars above earth. The lesson is in the sinking of the starfish into the mud in such a way so as not to lose contact with the stars:

> All at once they stopped,
> and as if they had simply
> increased their receptivity
> to gravity they sank down
> into the mud; they faded down
> into it and lay still; and by the time
> pink of sunset broke across them
> they were as invisible
> as the true stars at daybreak. (*MAMW,* 19)

Another successful lyric is "The Apple Tree." The more ordinary subject is more promising for successful closure in a shorter poem than are Kinnell's darker and more complex subjects. The poem is about a moment in the fall when the

> unfallen apples
> hold their brightness
> a little longer into the blue air, hold the dream
> they can be brighter. (*MAMW,* 65)

It is human nature to go on "until we touch the last flower of the last spring."

> When the fallen apple rolls
> into the grass, the apple worm
> stops, then goes
> all the way through and looks out
> at the creation unopposed, the world
> made entirely of lovers. (*MAMW,* 65)

The ultimate happiness depends on the willingness to continue to look out, knowing that an ending is a way of linking us with beginnings: "The one who holds still and looks out, / alone / of all of us, that one may die mostly of happiness" (*MAMW,* 66).

"The Milk Bottle" begins with a moment when

> A sea anemone
> sucks at my finger, mildly, I can just
> feel it, though it may mean to kill—no,
> it would probably say, to eat
> and flow . . . (*MAMW,* 67)

As of this moment Kinnell resists the flow, although he knows that "any time / would be OK / to go, to vanish back into all things," but the memory of another moment intervenes:

> I imagine I can actually remember one certain
> quart of milk which has just finished clinking
> against three of its brethren
> in the milkman's great hand and stands,
> freeing itself from itself, on the rotting
> doorstep in Pawtucket circa 1932. (*MAMW,* 67–68)

Again aware of time, he knows that the "Old milk bottle will shatter no one knows when" and "the sea eagle / will cry itself back down into the sea." In his own life, "Ahead of us the meantime is overflowing."

Death in The Family

The personal subjects continue to be essential, even those that go beyond the merely ordinary subject matter. Kinnell has returned in recent poems to the recurring subject of his dead brother. In "Brother of My Heart" he implies, as Lee Zimmerman has noted, a kind of poetic syllogism beginning with the major premise that identity is erased by death (Zimmerman, 203–4).

> Brother of my heart,
> don't you know there's only one
> walking into light, only one,
> before this light

> flashes out, before this bravest knight
> crashes his black bones into the earth? (*MAMW,* 12)

The minor premise is that nothing follows death. We live as human beings, only once. Worm life in the earth succeeds human life on the earth, the life of "moles or worms, / who grub into the first sorrow and lie there."

To counter this void, the major positive premise, and man's last word on the subject, can be expressed only from his penchant for song, to be celebrated in song even if that creative act is not quite sufficient compensation:

> sing, even if you cry; the bravery
> of the crying turns it into the true song; soul brother
> in heaven, on earth
> broken heart brother, sing to us
> here, in this place that loses its brothers,
> in this emptiness only the singing sometimes almost fills. (*MAMW,* 12)

"The Last Hiding Places of Snow" begins with memories of the sounds of his mother dying, leading him back in memory to thoughts about time in the womb. Kinnell is able to relate this primal experience to his later adult feelings of dread.

> and I knew, whenever I felt longings to go back,
> that is what wanting to die is. That is why
>
> dread lives in me,
> dread which comes when what gives life beckons toward death,
> dread which throws me
> waves
> of utter strangeness, which wash the entire world empty. (*MAMW,* 43)

Her dying "groans made / of all the goodbyes ever spoken" cause him to turn to the natural world, to "a place in the woods / where you can hear such sounds." And when he stops and listens he realizes:

> all I've heard was
> what may once have been speech
> or groans, now

shredded to a hiss from passing
through the whole valley of spruce needles. (*MAMW,* 42)

He perceives, mystifyingly, the presence of his mother there as in the falling snow.

in November, when a strange
starry perhaps first snowfall blows
down across the darkening air, lightly,
I know she is there, where snow
falls flakes down fragile softly
falling until I can't see the world
any longer, only its stilled shapes. (*MAMW,* 45)

"Flying Home"

The book's final poem, "Flying Home," utilizes the experience of flying back from Europe to America, but "flying home" also implicitly means returning to earth, from the sky to the more mundane, ordinary sphere that is our home:

As this plane dragging
its track of used ozone half the world long
thrusts some four hundred of us
toward places where actual known people
live and may wait,
we diminish down into our seats,
disappear into novels of lives clearer than ours,
and yet we do not forget for a moment
the life down there, the doorway each will soon enter:
where I will meet her again
and know her again,
dark radiance with, and then mostly without, the stars. (*MAMW,* 71)

Kinnell's recognition culminates in the knowledge that "love is very much like courage, / perhaps it *is* courage, and even / perhaps / only courage" (*MAMW,* 72). But then in the context established by these poems, courage is not a minor matter.

To compose a Rilkean book is no mean accomplishment for an American poet. It can even be considered major. To be able to sustain an ongoing meditation on time and mortality from a personal point of view is an important achievement for a postmodernist poet. If Kinnell's accomplishments in previous books of poetry seem to be on a grander scale, there are, nevertheless, little things in this volume that deserve attention, such as his little ironies, humor, even self-mockery. Most important though, Kinnell is now able to make meaningful poetry out of the ordinary things experienced in this life—a heron, blackberry eating, the apple tree, a milk bottle, a child falling from a tree, a child snuggling in with parents who have been making love, his continuing love for his dead brother. Harold Bloom, an authority on things Whitmanesque, in his rather unfavorable review of *Mortal Acts, Mortal Words,* judged that Galway Kinnell's descriptive powers were "increasing to a Whitmanesque amplitude" (Bloom, 109). Bloom should also have noted that this "Whitmanesque amplitude" is achieved impressively out of more personal and more ordinary things than were the subjects of Kinnell's poetry previously.

Lee Zimmerman also perceptively notes that Kinnell's style has undergone some modifications. His trademark had been fairly long sentences with "highly irregular lines" (Zimmerman, 199). This is noticeable and even bothersome. The sentence length has increased; but the former irregularities have been smoothed out, and there is now a greater sweep of the lines with much less resistance towards resolution. Kinnell has clearly tried to refashion his poetry. Sometimes it works, occasionally it does not. The question to raise now is where Galway Kinnell might go next.

Chapter Nine

The Past and Other Works

The Past Is Always the Past

Galway Kinnell's next book, *The Past* (1985), is a further venture into the short poem, resulting in 33 short poems in all. It is an ambitious endeavor with a substantial overall theme, reminding us in theme and in form that among Kinnell's poetic progenitors—in addition to Roethke and Rilke—was also Walt Whitman. *The Past* might fittingly be described as a series of short meditations on one of the most momentous topics for lyric poetry, worthy of Whitman—self and time. The poems are short, but the individual lines are variable, ranging from short to almost unmanageable Whitmanesque lengths. Kinnell states the theme he plays variations upon in the Whitmanesque opening poem, "The Road Between Here and There": "Here I sat on a boulder by the winter-steaming river and put my / head in my hands and considered time—which is next to / nothing, merely what vanishes, and yet can make one's elbows / nearly pierce one's thighs" (*TP,* 4).

It is the familiar places, the personal and private landmarks and the people associated with them that initiate the meditations. The particular place and the specific moment at which Kinnell begins his reflections on time and the effects of time on himself and on his friends is Sheffield, Vermont, more than 30 years ago. His consideration of time is a preference for the present moment, as is Rilke's; and his earlier meditations on life and death also owed much to that poet. In Rilke's poetic world the present physical world is often seen as potentially preferable to the heavenly one. Kinnell's rendering of this theme is that the present physical world may be superior to all remembered versions of the past one. The poems in *The Past* might be regarded simply as Kinnell's attempt to reconcile himself to the certitude that one cannot reenter past times since they are gone forever. The mood of these poems, from the first poem to the last, is one of acceptance of what is now. In the shortest poem of all, "Prayer," Kinnell writes: "Whatever happens. Whatever / *what is is is* what / I want. Only that. But that" (*TP,* 19).

And in the longest and the final poem, "The Seekonk Woods," Kinnell closes his meditation on time past and time present a bit more formally but with the same elegiac conclusion. He does suggest, though, that humankind may learn a new language, of which laughter is only the first stutter:

> The rails may never meet, O fellow Euclideans,
> for you, for me. So what if we groan?
> That's our noise. Laughter is our stuttering
> in a language we can't speak yet. Behind,
> the world made of wishes goes dark. Ahead,
> if not tomorrow then never, shines only what is. (*TP,* 57)

A meaningful response for Kinnell and the appropriate response for the poet that dwells in all of us is expression through song. The hope discovered in his previous book continues in this one. Individual singers or poets die, but the *singer* and the act of song will not die. In this respect human songs are one with the sounds and rhythms of nature, whether the elegies of birds or the shrill songs of the crickets. In "December Day in Honolulu," Kinnell interprets the wail of a cat in heat as meaning:

> This one or that one dies but never the singer: whether in Honolulu in its humid mornings or in New York in its unbreathable dusk or in Sheffield now dark but for chimney sparks dying into the crowded heaven, one singer falls but the next steps into the empty place and sings . . . (*TP,* 35)

"December Day in Honolulu" is short in lines, if long in line length; and it is actually one of Kinnell's most complex short poems. It opens with an informal, conversational comparison of day length in December in Honolulu and in Sheffield, Vermont. The longer day in the relative summer of Hawaii allows three separate postal deliveries that bring something relevant to the deaths of three poets, James Wright, Muriel Rukeyser, and Robert Hayden. The objects that stir him to thought are the four glass doorknobs "sea-mailed" to him by Muriel Rukeyser, activating from the past memories of the words she used to whisper whenever they met, "Galway, I have your doorknobs" (*TP,* 35).

Kinnell has explained the passage as referring to an often forgotten promise on the part of Rukeyser to give him some doorknobs, something that she always forgot to do until after ten years he received proof that she had, at last, remembered. "Then finally they arrived in the mail, and I remembered that she had promised to give me these doorknobs. They were pure glass" (*BWR,* 181–82).

In one of his most personal poems, "On the Oregon Coast," Kinnell confronts the deaths of two of his poet friends—Richard Hugo and James Wright. He begins with some very effective descriptive details which set an appropriate scene:

Six or seven rows of waves struggle landward.
The wind batters a pewtery sheen on the water between them.
As each wave makes its way in, most of it gets blown back out to
 sea, subverting even necessity.
The bass rumble of sea stones, audible when the waves flee all
 broken back out to sea, itself blows out to sea.
Now a log maybe thirty feet long and six across gets up and
 trundles down the beach.
Like a dog fetching a stick it flops unhesitatingly into the water. (*TP,* 36)

Kinnell's use of personification leads him to recall that the last time he was on this beach he had a conversation on the subject of personification with his friend and fellow poet Richard Hugo at a restaurant just north of his present location. The conclusion from their dialogue was that "as post-Darwinians it was up to us to anthropomorphize / the world less and animalize, vegetablize, and mineralize our- / selves more." But "We doubted that pre-Darwinian language would let us." They remembered a poet friend whose closeness to nature, rather than the customary separation, marked an exception to this restriction and directed their attention ". . . to James Wright, how his kinship with salaman- / ders, spiders and mosquitoes allowed him to drift back down / through the evolutionary stages" (*TP,* 36).

Kinnell is sadly cognizant that both of these poets have gone on to the final event. Yet, though their physical presence is gone into the past, the present scene remains the same.

The waves coming in burst up through their crests and fly very
 brilliant back out to sea.
The log gets up again, goes rolling and bouncing down the
 beach, plunges as though for good into the water. (*TP,* 37)

In a second poem on the subject of dead poets, "Last Holy Fragrance," Kinnell again summons up from the past, another time, another place, in Vence, France. This was the moment in "the last house on the Chemin de Riou," where the poet James Wright was "mumbling into his notebook at an upstairs window" (*TP,* 38). The very next winter, back in St. Paul, Minnesota, Wright handed Kinnell the finished poem he had begun on that day. Now whenever Kinnell tries to read it for himself, he hears Wright's voice; and the poem has the same emotional effect on him that he remembered it having on the occasion of the poet himself reading "when the poems were at their saddest." He perceives that it is the song that takes over the poet's reading, since "poetry sings past even the sadness / that begins it." This circumstance happens because all readings of poems seek "that chant of the beginning, / older than any poem" (*TP,* 39). He also recognizes that laughter can win through the suffering. He recalls an old James Cagney World War Two movie *The House on Rue Madeline,* when Cagney, under torture by the Gestapo, hears the rumbling of the B–24s "come to shut his mouth." When "the bombs start exploding about him, / he throws back his head and madly laughs" (*TP,* 39–40). Such an ending is plausible for James Wright's poem or, by implication, for Kinnell's own effort. Kinnell's poem ends, not sadly but formally, emotion under control, a closure that suggests that this is almost Kinnell's pastoral elegy for his own Lycidas or Adonais:

> He went away,
> three-quarters whittled root of silenus wood,
> taking a path that, had it simply vanished,
> we could imagine keeps going, toward a place
> where he waits—in winding-cloth or swaddling-sheet. (*TP,* 40–41)

The death of the poet is lamentable because the loss of talent is for a time irreplaceable. "It will be a long time before anyone comes / who can lull the words" as James Wright could (*TP,* 41). But as a poet himself, Kinnell knows that what becomes important with the passage in time is the song itself: the words Wright has left behind will certify that the song and, through it, the singer will endure. In "Last Holy Fragrance," it should also be noted, Kinnell documents from his memories of the past the struggle of a poet to say the unsayable:

> But poetry sings past even the sadness
> that begins it: the drone of poetry readings

> or the mutterings coming from poets' workrooms—
> as oblivious to emotion as the printed page—(*TP,* 38)

Kinnell remembers the poet's requisite question and complaint in one of the most emotive statements in contemporary poetry on the difficulty of reaching what poets strive to accomplish.

> "How am I ever going to be able to say this?
> The truth is there is something terrible,
> almost unspeakably terrible in our lives,
> and it demands respect, and, for some reason
> that seems to me quite insane, it doesn't hate us.
> There, you see? Every time I try
> to write it down it comes out gibberish." (*TP,* 39)

Among the poems in *The Past* is another longer but significant political poem, "The Fundamental Project of Technology," a worthy addition to Kinnell's small but significant gathering of political poems expressing his awareness that, in the nuclear world, modern technology has created a threat even at the only place where the past actually survives—in human consciousness. In Nagasaki, Kinnell visits the museum commemorating the dropping in that city of the second and the last atomic bomb on human targets. He witnesses relics on display that in one way or another survived that terrible destruction. These are simple, ordinary things from a human world but "changed as our world is changed." Kinnell is remarkably graphic in his use of things, in his realization of physical objects in these poems.

> Under glass: glass dishes which changed
> in color; pieces of transformed beer bottles;
> a household iron; bundles of wire become solid
> lumps of iron; a pair of pliers; a ring of skull-
> bone fused to the inside of a helmet; a pair of eyeglasses
> taken off the eyes of an eyewitness, without glass,
> which vanished, when a white flash sparkled. (*TP,* 47)

As he scrutinizes how even these items were transformed by the destructive power of nuclear technology, Kinnell realizes that the fundamental project of such technology is "To de-animalize human mentality, to purge it of obsolete / evolutionary characteristics, in particular of death," making it essential "to eliminate those who die" (*TP,* 48). This is what has happened to the children; they are gone, but they live horribly in the memory "in scorched uniforms, holding tiny crushed lunch tins." There they will live at least as long as human consciousness survives, "until the day flashes and no one lives / to look back and say, a flash, a white flash sparkled" (*TP,* 48).

In the title poem, "The Past," undoubtedly one of his best poems of the 1980s, Kinnell returns as an older poet to a scene where he spent some time many years before as a young poet. He recalls now the particulars of his writing environment then. The process of writing continues even though the objects he remembers from that past as associated with it are gone:

> A chair under one arm,
> a desktop under the other,
> the same Smith-Corona
> on my back I even now batter
> words into visibility with,
> I would walk miles,
> assemble my writing stall,
> type all day, many sheets
> of prose and verse all blown
> away, while herring gulls
> and once a sightseeing plane
> turned overhead. (*TP,* 42)

Kinnell can, in the present, distinguish only remnants of that past, a lean-to made of driftwood that he had put up on this spot, "thirty-three and a third years back." Other things are gone, like the quonset hut he broke into, which he had wanted very much to be there still. The waves remind him of the effect of time, which with the experience of a third of a century behind him, he now sees as "mere comings, mere goings . . . Though now there's somewhat less coming / in the comings and considerably more / going in the goings." He decides, with an effective figure for what he perceives:

> So you see,
> to reach the past is easy. A snap.
> A snap of the sea and a third of a century
> passes. All nothing. Or all all,

> if that sounds more faithful. But anyway
> all gone. . . . (*TP,* 44)

Like most writers contemplating the past Kinnell would like to return to the times that have vanished. He has to reconcile himself to the reality that except for glimpses the past is always the past, never actually the present; he lives in the here and now, having to reconcile himself to the fundamental truth that life with the passage of time becomes deprivation. Even to pray to have something is through that very act to acknowledge that one can never have full possession of it. In the poem "The Past" Kinnell is probing what he described in "The Road between Here and There" as "For here, the moment all the spaces along the road between here / and there—which the young know are infinite and all the others / know are not" (*TP,* 4). He can remember when it all seemed to be infinite, but he is unmistakably now one who knows that it is not; he is merely finite. His poems lament, but also sanction, this knowledge that time has given.

The poem "Middle of the Night" intermingles past and present, with memories back to his boyhood friends Kenny Hardeman and George Sykes calling "'Gaw-way-ay!' at the back / of the house. If I didn't come out / they would call until nightfall, like summer insects" (*TP,* 6). But this memory poem of the past is also a poem of the present. "A telephone rings through the wall. / Nobody answers . . ." "Or like / the pay phone at the abandoned / filling station, which sometimes / rang, off and on, an entire day" (*TP,* 6). This is a poem also about the shapes the mouth assumes saying things of value like "gold" or "yes" as the "final yawn before one sleeps," or the impossibility of walking away from the affirmative eyes of a woman or being insensitive enough to bewilder "a mouth making the last yawn to say 'no.'"

There is a also a memory from the past revived in the family poem "The Olive Wood Fire." It is of a time when Fergus "woke crying at night" and Kinnell "would carry him from his crib / to the rocking chair and sit holding him / before the fire of thousand-year-old olive wood" (*TP,* 9). In contrast to his memory as a father holding the son, he has the nightmarish dream or thought that he heard something from out of the violence of the past, from the terrible war in Vietnam, "a scream / —a flier crying out in horror / as he dropped fire on he didn't know what or whom, / or else a child thus set aflame—." Fortunately, he returns from this dream of past horrors among America's nightmares to the love he has for his son in the present: "The olive wood fire / had burned low. In my arms lay Fergus, / fast asleep, left cheek glowing, God" (*TP,* 9).

With the restorative power emanating from this scene of parental love he can, from the father's side of happiness, now add the final word, "God." In his most recent interview Kinnell comments in some detail on his use of the word "God" in this poem in reference to his son:

> The word God is a word I don't use very often. I use it sometimes because there isn't actually another word which will do. I use it as a metaphor. I'm not saying that he [Fergus] is some kind of supreme being, but rather he is at that moment in my eyes the embodiment of the sacred character of life. For that embodiment we won't have many words unless we want to talk about the sacred, the "embodiment of the sacred," and so forth, which is very hard, clumsy, and abstract. (*BWR,* 173–74)

Poems in *The Past* tend to achieve poetic closure on words of affirmation. In "Conception" a man and woman end intercourse with the woman asserting the value of the continuance of human life and of the nuclear family: "'Yes, I am two now, / and with thee, three'" (*TP,* 7). Even in a supplement to his poetic bestiary, in a further animal poem, there is a humorous confirmation of this value. In "The Sow Piglet's Escapes" the escaped pig seems to signal a reminder that she must be caught and returned to the safety of her home:

> as if to remind me not to forget to recapture her—though, really, a pig's special alertness to death ought to have told her: in Sheffield the *dolce vita* leads to the Lyndonville butcher. But when I seized her she wriggled hard and cried, *wee wee wee,* all the way home. (*TP,* 8)

Kinnell's concern with time is primarily with memories of the past, but he cannot exclude consideration of the future. In "First Day of the Future" he knows that the "cold earthly dawns" of the future are just an illusion. It is "just another day they illuminate / of the permanent present." He is aware of everything, and imagines others, that separate him from this past. Nevertheless he can still imagine it and he determines:

> I don't know about this new life.
> Even though I burned the ashes of its flag again and again

and set fire to the ticket that might have conscripted me into its
ranks forever,
even though I have squandered all my talents composing my emigra-
tion papers,
I think I want to go back now and live again in the present time,
back there
when someone milks a cow and jets of intensest nourishment go
squawking into a pail (*TP,* 45)

Having dealt with his memories of the past, Kinnell concludes that his life must be in the present. Nevertheless, in order to maintain hope and meaning, he must find himself living in the future, or so he imagines. He concludes:

But I guess I'm here. So I must take care. For here
one has to keep facing the right way, or one sees one dies, and
one dies.
I'm not sure I'm going to like it living here in the future.
I don't think I can keep on doing it indefinitely. (*TP,* 45–46)

"First Day of the Future" is different, as are many poems in *The Past.* In commenting on Robert Frost's condemnation of free verse as like playing tennis with the net down, Kinnell contended that this image showed that poetry was a game to Frost, whereas in his own view poetry was not a game but a journey (*PPW,* 114). The description is apt for both poets. The journey for Kinnell was often a bleak and dark journey. Perhaps writing poetry has recently taken on some of the aspects of a game also for Kinnell with the discernment that playfulness is not an indication of a lack of seriousness. The seriousness depends on the significance of the subjects he explores. Kinnell's subjects are still serious; but there now seems to be more of an element of play evident to accompany somewhat stronger notes of affirmation, if what is reached is not quite yet celebration. What is more crucial is that in *The Past* Kinnell touches real life by including more actual places, especially with the objects his memory salvages from the past in Sheffield, Vermont. There are also memories of people not just his family, but also his friends, his fellow poets. Kinnell has continued to populate his poems with real people. His friends may be dead, but what seems decisive in this book is that they fulfilled their functions by the way they lived. For the poet there is a great danger in writing poems on the past, and Kinnell also acknowledges this danger in his poems on that subject. He recalls in "The Past" a letter from his friend and mentor, not named, but no doubt Charles Bell, with a warning: "Don't lose / all touch with humankind" (*TP,* 43). Kinnell doesn't, really. His command of physical details permits him to keep meaningful contact with the past, although it is the past. And in the present he has his family and other living poet friends. He is still concerned with mortality; but in these poems of the 1980s, at some distance from the events of the 1960s, he is also aware of consciousness, of awareness itself. Humor is more evident. Kinnell seems to be learning "the stutter of laughter" well enough for it to become a new and developing poetic language for him. It is a development not predictable from his earliest poetry. He has learned an appreciation for the incongruities of life and the eccentricities of people, as the refrain in this poem, "Galway, I have your doorknobs," announces. Galway Kinnell has consciously given his reader an often idiosyncratic view of the world in this book. The poems may not consistently come up to his usual standards. But one should appreciate the difference this book sanctions.

In 1987 Galway Kinnell edited a little book that is appropriate for his interests as a poet and to his knowledge as a critic, a selected edition of Whitman, *The Essential Whitman.*[1] The short introduction is a personal account of what Walt Whitman has meant to him from his first days of reading Whitman in high school and in college through his career as a fellow poet. The turning point from appreciation to influence resulted from his teaching Whitman at the University of Grenoble as a Fulbright lecturer when Kinnell was in his late twenties. "Under Whitman's spell I stopped writing in rhyme and meter and in rectangular stanzas and turned to long-lined, loosely cadenced verse; and at once I felt immensely liberated. . . . Whitman has been my principal master ever since" (*EW,* 3). Kinnell's selection of poems for his own edition comes from personal favorites.

The main problem for him as an editor was what to do about Whitman's later revisions of his poetry. The mistake Whitman made was to forget that his poetry was not just about himself, "but about a representative man, a workman-poet." Whitman's error is obviously one that Kinnell wishes to avoid himself. He wants to take care that his persona, while in the process of becoming more personal, must not become as personal and as subjectively introspective or as confessional as personae have in so much of recent American poetry. For Whitman the changes in his poetic persona were "destructive changes," as they would be for Kinnell as a poet. Kinnell, though, has maintained his discipline. His poems may have grown more personal, especially with the advent of family poems; but they are always designed as representative.

When One Has Lived a Long Time Alone

In Galway Kinnell's tenth major book of poetry, *When One Has Lived a Long Time Alone,* which appeared in late 1990 from a new publisher, Alfred A. Knopf, he confronts his own solitariness from other people, including family, and ultimately that terminal loneliness, his own mortality. A key line in the volume might well be "everything sings and dies," but it could also be "everything dies and sings," the decisive perception from "Flower of Five Blossoms" (*WOHLLTA,* 52). Dying is a characteristic humankind share with other creatures, but singing is a resource that the poet finds in people. In these poems Kinnell writes of loss, separation, death, aloneness after the breakup of the family he has celebrated in the antecedent poems. His trademark, the long poem, appears; but he also shows his ability to complete and master the short poem.

When One Has Lived a Long Time Alone contains 22 poems, divided into four parts, the first three with seven poems each, and the fourth part consisting entirely of the long title poem, "When One Has Lived a Long Time Alone." Three of the shorter poems strike me as especially fine, "Judas-Kiss," "The Cat," and "The Perch." I would also praise the shortest poem in the volume, doubtless Kinnell's shortest ever good poem (a scant seven lines), "Divinity." Love is, once again, the only assurance against loneliness. In this poem Kinnell designates the ultimate escape from aloneness as that intimacy consummated with "the woman" at the moment he "touches through to the exact center" and "his loving friend becomes his divinity" (*WOHLLTA,* 46). In "The Vow," his second shortest poem, consisting of eight brief lines, the lover leaves but their vow, "though broken," remains as a trace of eternal love "to give dignity to the suffering / and to intensify it" (*WOHLLTA,* 43).

Kinnell's tone is appropriately somber and reflective, for poems that disclose that love ends in suffering; but in "Oatmeal," where Kinnell imagines sharing a bowl of porridge with John Keats, a rare, but welcome, show of humor occurs: "I am aware it is not good to eat oatmeal alone. / Its consistency is such that it is better for your mental health if / somebody eats it with you" (*WOHLLTA*, 37). The oatmeal-eating Keats confesses that two of his best lines from "To Autumn," which he recites, came to him "while eating oatmeal alone." The knowledge that both poets share, romantic and postmodern, is that poems, the natural tendency to sing, can result from being alone.

The title poem, "When One Has Lived a Long Time Alone," specifies the loneliness of living by oneself as so potent that to retain the presence of another he hesitates to swat the fly or to strike the mosquito, and even lifts the toad "from the pit too deep to hop out of," and helps the swift stunned from crashing into the glass to "fly free" (*WOHLLTA*, 59). For companionship he may even grab the snake behind the head, hold him, and observe him. Or he may listen at morning to "mourning doves / sound their *kyrie eleison*" (*WOHLLTA*, 64). He, "as the conscious one," being human becomes the consciousness for the live creatures of nature around him, the red-headed woodpecker, "clanging out his music / from a metal drainpipe," or the grouse drumming his sound from deep in the woods (*WOHLLTA*, 65). He even relishes the "unlikeables" of nature—the pig, the porcupine—and with a touch of misanthropic loneliness he confesses that "one finds one likes / any other species better than one's own" (*WOHLLTA*, 66). "Sour, misanthropic," he momentarily accepts the loneliness of forgetting one's own kind. But this mood passes, and the conclusive lesson from these denizens of nature is that one mates with one's own kind and his prayer becomes a wish to revert to one's own kind, "to live again among men and women" and to come back "to that place where one's ties with the human / broke" where lovers speak and stand "in a halo of being made one" (*WOHLLTA*, 69).

There are poems of the loneliness of memory, the memories of his father and of his wife. The seven-part "Memories of My Father" counters his feeling of aloneness by contending that "Those we love from the first / can't be put aside or forgotten, / after they die they still must be cried / out of existence" (*WOHLLTA*, 11). He will return to the house and to memories of his father, and he expects to stop to hear someone singing whether it is his father or "someone I don't know." Kinnell still believes in the continuation of the act of singing, of the poignant human importance of giving form to one's feelings.

Another memory poem needed to sing his father out of existence, "Kilauea," bears the name of the Hawaiian volcano and opens with an image of a stone found with two holes in it, which recalls a skull. He is reminded of his father's brow and of his "sprinting to get to death / before his cares could catch up / and kill him" (*WOHLLTA,* 6). A small rainbow forms around him, its two ends almost touching his feet. He wonders if he could consequently be the pot of gold at the end of the rainbow. The poem ends with two memories of his father: the first of him in the cellar shoveling in "a new utopia of coal," delivering clanking noises to the radiator pipes; the second stropping his razor and shaving in the bathroom, hooting out "last night's portion of disgust" in song (*WOHLLTA,* 7).

"The Auction" begins with the aloneness of the poet whose sleeping wife "lies in another dream," covered by a quilt "like a hill / of neat farms" (*WOHLLTA,* 12), and moves on to his own dreams about the chest "the color of blood / spilled long ago" sold at auction with the instruction that "*All the old love letters go with it, all go*!" Though the words live on, the lovers lie asleep "in the scythed, white-fenced precinct / on the Heights," with "their alphabets / now two scatterings of bones" (*WOHLLTA,* 14). "The Massage" contrasts the intimacy of the physical contact of the body and the two busy hands of the massager—"How could anyone / willingly leave a world where they touch you / all over your body?" (*WOHLLTA,* 16)—and the distractions of external world sounds, including the urgent sound of an ambulance or police siren that leads to thoughts of cadavers on a slab and their last massage in preparation for the funeral. "The Man on the Hotel Room Bed" is a grim picture of night loneliness: "He feels around— / no pillow next to his, no depression / in the pillow, no head in the depression" (*WOHLLTA,* 20). The only consolation for his solitariness is that alone he cannot be abandoned. This is "a man lying alone to avoid being abandoned, / who wants to die to escape the meeting with death" (*WOHLLTA,* 21).

"Agape" contrasts a man's desire to touch a woman and a patient willingness to wait until he can be instructed by a priestess "on love rightly understood" (*WOHLLTA,* 31). He realizes that, as time passes, like all things, she will age and yet he is fearful of what the test of touch may reveal: "I don't want / to know that on the other / side of the pillow nobody / stirs" (*WOHLLTA,* 32).

There are poems on other women, actual and perhaps mythological. "Who, on Earth" is both a discovery of a skate, lying on the sand of a beach, sucking holes, and a vivid waking dream, with the vision of a woman, mermaid-like, "up to her waist in a pool, / singing" (*WO-*

HLLTA, 33). The skate, dying, presses down into the sand, "trying to fall into heaven / inside earth" but is overwhelmed by the force of the waves that inevitably drag off its carcass, "leaving bubbles which pop" (*WOHLLTA,* 34). An analogy is made with the boy harangued by his mother and "icy-shouldered" by his father who "can only fall in loneliness / with . . . but . . . who, / on earth?" (*WOHLLTA,* 35).

"The Cat," which appeared as Kinnell's contribution to the "Fortieth Anniversary Issue" of the *Beloit Poetry Journal,* is indirectly a personal story about his interest in, as his host announces, "someone . . . a woman in your life. . . ."[2] But his concern is fixed on the treatment of the cat: "It is an awful thing you are doing. . . . When you lock her up / she becomes dangerous" (*WOHLLTA,* 26). It is both a cat and yet, in consequence, a mythological creature so that neither he nor his host can let it know its effect on them. Both he and his host are seized as if by "an electric force." His hands "flopping at his sides," while his host pretends, "I am washing the dishes":

> I realize that he is trying to make the cat to believe
> he is not in a seizure but washing the dishes.
> If either of us lets on about the seizure
> I know for certain the cat will kill us both. (*WOHLLTA,* 26)

In one of two *New Yorker* poems, "The Perch,"[3] there is once more the memory of a woman friend and of a favorite perspective, "a fork in a branch / of an ancient, enormous maple," for looking out "over miles of valleys and low hills" (*WOHLLTA,* 41). Later, accompanied on skis by the woman, he concentrates on the trunk of the tree "contoured by the terrible struggles of that time when it had its hard time," aware "that some such time now comes upon me." He hears a rifle fired several times and regards this sound as

> percussions
> of the custom of male mastery
> over the earth—the most graceful,
> most alert, most gentle of the animals
> being chosen to die. (*WOHLLTA,* 42).

The poem concludes with the grace of a glance, as the woman "looked up—the way, from low / to high, the god blesses. . . ."

Kinnell sustains in the context of these poems his former preoccupation with time. In the second *New Yorker* poem, "Judas-Kiss,"[4] he knows that it "goes away eventually," once in a while "skips a day," even "a whole year can get lost." But time "basically sits there" (*WOHLLTA,* 18). The only way to rush the process of departing is through death. For this finality there will be a human recognition, a sign of shared humanity, even if what is bestowed is by the nature of death's solitariness, a false Judas kiss.

> Then somebody,
> an ex-spouse, the woman downstairs,
> or maybe the UPS man, will happen by,
> discover the collapsed creature,
> and, never mind if it sleeps through
> its last clutches, bend down,
> and with the softest
> part of the face, which hides
> the hardest, Judas-kiss it,
> with a click, like a conductor's
> ticket punch, this one here, God
> of our Fathers, this one is the one. (*WOHLLTA,* 18–19)

"Farewell" is a poem based on Haydn's "Farewell Symphony," during the performance of which musicians in ones or twos gradually fold up their music and depart. It is a superb musical metaphor for poems concerned with aloneness and thoughts of mortality.

> The orchestra disappears—
> by ones, the way we wash up on the unmusical shore,
> and by twos, the way we enter the ark where the world goes on
> beginning. (*WOHLLTA,* 53)

As the last two violinists remain "who have figured out what / they have figured out by sounding it upon the other," he sees the face of his old departed friend Paul Zweig, "—who went away, his powers intact, into Eternity's Woods alone" (*WOHLLTA,* 54).

Kinnell can be personal and yet suggestively archetypal, and, surprisingly, he can achieve a felt communication of something significant even in the short lyric, a matter that used to cause him some difficulty. The most significant development in his recent poetry is a matter of intensity.

Galway Kinnell no longer believes that everything in his poetry must burn with the fierce flames of intensity. More ordinary human life as a subject has the consequence of getting the feel of a warmer humanity into the poems. Death remains a key subject, but here it is the deaths of contemporaries, of friends, of fellow poets, and contemplation of his own approaching death. But the subject is no longer quite as solemn. To follow up on "December Day in Honolulu" the wail of a cat can be interpreted as communicating the continuity of the cat's "wail" or the poet's song as revealing that "one singer falls but the next steps into the empty place and sings" (*TP,* 35). There is a calmer acceptance, not necessarily of anything momentous but of anything, everything.

Kinnell, the Master Translator

No statement about Kinnell's importance as a poet would be complete without a tribute to his abilities as a translator. His translation of *The Poems of François Villon* is a major venture into the genre.[5] He translates not only two long poems, "The Legacy" and "The Testament," but also fifteen of the shorter poems. Kinnell makes it clear that he was not attempting the popular "imitations" of the 1960s when a poet of that decade tried to express in his own voice the thoughts and forms of another time and place. What Robert Lowell and others were attempting were truly imitations in the sense of doing one's own thing with another poet's subject, whereas what is important to Kinnell is accuracy to another time and to another language. But his interest in translating comes from the fact that we "really do want to know as much as we can of what a poet in some other time or place actually thought and felt" (*WDS,* 12). His attraction to Villon, a poet of five centuries ago, must have come from that poet's unsentimental look at the harsh physical realities in urban life of those times. Kinnell undoubtedly wanted to catch from that poet some of the effects he wanted in his own poetry. He does it remarkably well. From this volume one can learn both about Villon's poetry and Galway Kinnell's.

Chapter Ten

Conclusion for Now

It is not really possible to reach a conclusion on a poet whose work is still very much in progress and from whom a new book of poetry is expected momentarily. It is feasible only to make judgments as to the significance of what Kinnell has written so far and to estimate what the most recent work hints about future directions. By the 1980s, as a winner of both the Pulitzer Prize and the American Book Award for poetry, Galway Kinnell had at last received public recognition for what was known privately by a few critics and fellow poets—that he is one of our most talented poets. He had at last achieved critical acclaim without ever acquiring a substantial popular reputation, although his publisher assures that his books of poetry have always sold.

Kinnell is respected for having written much serious and striking meditative poetry without being granted much credit for achieving lyric grace; however, as I have tried to show, there was always some measure of lyricism. And there are a number of good lyric poems among the shorter poems in his last two volumes of poetry. Kinnell's poems are also personal, as most postmodernist poetry must be read, in the sense that he is usually recognizable as the protagonist of his own poems involved in whatever narrative the poem implies. He has featured his own family but never sensationally or sentimentally. His poems are never confessional to the melodramatic extent that poems by Lowell, Berryman, or Plath were. If I have been able to show that Kinnell's poems can be personal in subject and lyrical in style and that he writes poems on significant themes, there is still a complication. Critics seem to agree that his poems may have a recognizable persona but that they usually fail to convey much sense of a distinctive or even recognizable voice. Galway Kinnell's poems tend to be recognizable rather for their subject matter. Language poets are currently downplaying the importance of voice, but its importance still remains with critics as a legacy of the New Criticism. In the context of the last 30 years of postmodernist poetry, this deficiency—if it can be called a deficiency—can be a matter of some import.

In the eye of some critical beholders, there has also been a difficulty with Kinnell's themes. Harold Bloom has complained that everything Kinnell deals with in poetry has to be a crucial event. I would tend to agree in part. In some of his most characteristic books, the reader may indeed feel a desire to advise Kinnell to "lighten up." In Kinnell's poetic terrain, it may be difficult to distinguish among his mountains because there are very few valleys to highlight them. In 1975 Richard Eberhart similarly referred to Kinnell's unrelenting look at the truth in his poetry (Howard Nelson, 136). To some readers this look has been too unrelenting, too gloomy, too literally dead serious, but to others, a source of great power.

The terrain of Galway Kinnell's poetry still is well travelled. By the time he was writing the poems collected in *Body Rags,* the poet had seemingly determined that nature was the most appropriate and effective scene for the drama of his poems. These nature scenes, the settings for his version of the archetypal romantic encounter between persona and some aspect of nature, are vividly and graphically presented. A characteristic Kinnell poem features a journey through an impressively established scene in nature on the way to a meditation on important questions, disclosing a solicitude for the life-death interfaces, his own and everyone's and even everything else's.

While Kinnell has sought to be personal, he has also wanted to be universal, to turn his persona into everyman. When this effort becomes too labored, the poems lose some of their great intensity. Still, I agree with James Dickey that Kinnell usually communicates better when he is personal; however, I acknowledge, as Dickey does not allow, that there are exceptions as in the great animal poems, "The Porcupine" and "The Bear." In the latter the persona and not the poet is impersonal, apparently an Eskimo; and the poem is clearly one of his most intensified. The animals make the difference. It is also characteristic that these successful poems are long poems, not short lyrics. Kinnell is known for his long poems, and he should be given credit for how he is able to build up and maintain intensity in these poems.

Galway Kinnell's poems are designed to sound significant; usually they do, especially when his own readings consummate their auditory potentials before live audiences. When Kinnell reads, there is no problem with hearing a distinctive voice. His poems are perceptibly written to be read aloud, and the best way to read them is to let the poem take over, as the poet seems to do in his own readings. Kinnell comes across best through his strenuously evocative diction and in the often powerful rhetoric of his longer meditative poems. He can, however, overreach, and in some of his less successful poems be justifiably accused of producing a "strained rhetoric." To write at his best, Kinnell requires concreteness, a focus on the particularity of the world before he goes off "slogging for the absolute." Charles Altieri, not necessarily the most friendly critic to Kinnell's kind of verse, is convinced that Kinnell is not often able to "sustain and to resolve the level of intense, theatricalized suffering of the poem's often brilliant nightmare vision." Altieri believes that Kinnell is just not quite able to "elaborate a metaphysical scene equal to his demonic moments" (Howard Nelson, 139). At least he is given credit for creating "demonic moments," not a minor achievement for a contemporary poet. Altieri's view is not entirely fair. There are good "metaphysical scenes" in Kinnell, and I have tried to show that he does not always need an elaborate metaphysical scene for a successful poem.

It is helpful to see Kinnell in relation to his great predecessors, most obviously Rilke; less obviously, but still decisively, in relation to Theodore Roethke. If we are to judge Kinnell's success in terms of his intentions, it is essential to know that Kinnell took seriously Roethke's advice to the lyric poet to be "compelling and immediate," for at his best he is exactly that—"compelling" and "immediate." It is also easy to know his intentions because he has usually stated them in one of his rather numerous interviews. Kinnell is demonstrably better at stringing out an imagistic structure than at plotting narratives or providing narrative frames for his meditations. His poems proceed by image patterns and are organized by oppositions, which customarily means that he is effective in pairing off terms for life and death, extinction and renewal in his poetry. Various critics have used a variety of terms in identifying a kind of "pervasive binarism" in his language as well as in his themes, described as "variations on individual words," "double meanings," or "the resonance of words." Poststructuralist critics who believe these to be basic structures in poetry should relish exploring this poet's "binary oppositions." In his paired imagery of death and life, Kinnell explores all of their variant meanings, positive and negative.

It should also be recognized that if Kinnell lacks humor, his poems are sporadically saved from pretentiousness by an attitude of ironic self-deprecation, a characteristic more evident in his recent poems than it was in his earlier ones. A careful reading of Kinnell will reveal that not all of his poems are, after all, inevitably momentous metaphysical journeys. It is just that these are among his better known. Kinnell gives us the world honestly as he saw it at that moment; and in the telling of his vision, it may often appear rather melodramatic. It should be noted, however, that he never overstates the impact of his own importance on that world. He is personal but restricted by his dedication to speaking not solely for himself but for all who are living creatures.

It has been said that Kinnell's setting is typically a scene in nature, a journey up a mountain, or down a wilderness road—the archetypally romantic scene of nature established as a place for a significant encounter or insight or for posing questions of ultimate concern. This establishes that he is a good nature poet, but he is not exclusively one; there are urban poems with an international range from New York City to Calcutta, or town poems set in smaller communities like Westport, Connecticut, and Sheffield, Vermont. He has actually written perhaps the finest, surely the best-known, of post–World War Two urban poems, "The Avenue Bearing the Initial of Christ into the New World." When his setting is nature, it is never static. It is often a scene of activity. His persona is engaged in the activities of walking beaches, climbing mountains, encountering in the wilderness animals that he recognizes share his own vulnerability. Kinnell may even on occasion romantically meditate over ruins, stare up at the starry night sky. This is all fashionable postmodernist neoromanticism with more than a touch of 1950s existential ultimate concern.

Galway Kinnell should be grouped, as David Perkins correctly sees him, among those poets who have been enticed to turn against the civilization that Western man has formed (Perkins, 553). After all, civilization in his poetry is represented rather consistently by destructive products of technology—by a SAC jet bomber leaving a vapor trail, or by the confused and purposeless lives of his urban residents, whether on Avenue C in New York City, or in the slums of Calcutta. Nevertheless, in such a world there is an important role for the poet as the singer, and an even more significant place for the poem he writes, the song he sings. Human song should be cognate to the songs of nature—expressive of nature's rhythms as heard in the cracking movements of quilled porcupines, in the heavy, noisy lumbering of bears, in the small shrill songs of crickets. All of these creatures are common participants in the life energy that also "burns," becoming in time the destructive as well as the nurturing fires of life. In such a world, poetry, order, form is necessary. Song is one of the human gestures, including the embrace, important to Kinnell's exemplar Whitman and to his own poetry. What compensates in his life-death interface, Kinnell's poetry shows us, are such acts as the child snuggling in the bed of his lovemaking parents, tributes to a dead brother, and other acts of love that establish the bonds of human meaning in a bleak naturalistic world. Galway Kinnell is, after all, a humanist.

Kinnell should be viewed as an important neoromantic also for the distinctive kind of mythic primitivism intrinsic to his poetry as part of what Perkins has classified as his anticivilization pose. He not only writes poems featuring primitive scenes—his mountain climbing out alone, his camping out solitary in the wilderness during the winter—but he also dramatizes primal violations of the "one life" principle—his killing a bird to be eaten at Christmas dinner, or on a grander scale, his shooting buffalo with a murderer for his companion. For such violations a propitiatory act is necessary. Such poetry is unusual for our times and inherently interesting for the obvious reason that violations of nature, such as the killing of whales or of dolphins, are now part of great environmental solicitude. As a poet who desires nature for itself, Kinnell wants to address that tendency in all of us to control and dominate nature and all the rest of life. He has stated his position very well in *Walking Down the Stairs*.

> I suppose that in human societies from the beginning, there was both a drive to control and to dominate the rest of life, and also a desire to be one with the rest. These opposing urges must have been in reasonable balance, often both must have been present in the same act, of hunting, cultivation, propitiation, and so on. Since the Renaissance the drive to dominate has won out. (*WDS,* 18)

Unmistakably, more attention should also be given to Kinnell as a poetic craftsman. What he had to learn as one educated in the modernism of T. S. Eliot and the formalism of the New Criticism was to put aside formalist and modernist doctrine, to abandon formal stanzas and meters for a freer verse; at the same time, he had to avoid the romantic diction that had been used traditionally to express his kind of ideas. In his later poetry Kinnell has varied the length of his lines dramatically, sometimes changing the number of syllables in a line from a minimum of two to a maximum of twenty. He is demonstrably a superb craftsman, whether in his earlier formalist mode or in his later free verse, open-form manner. Still, the considerable craft behind many of his best poems has not been admired sufficiently, perhaps from the assumption that if his poetry lacks variety in theme, it must also be deficient in method. On the contrary, there is a richly perceptible music to be heard in Kinnell's poems, rich patterns of sounds so far not fully heard by his critics.

Galway Kinnell may not yet be a master of the short lyric, but he is surely one of our best craftsmen in producing medium-long postmodernist versions of the renaissance meditative poem or the great romantic ode. The meditation has been recognized among his forms; his approaches to the ode have not been acknowledged. Kinnell must be given due consideration in any study of the long poem in modern American poetry, a genre in which there is considerable current critical interest. He has been remarkably successful in building up long poems through shorter poems written as sections of a long poem. In this respect, he is most like his great mentor Rilke, whose *Duino Elegies* he has imitated with success in *The Book of Nightmares,* in the 1960s fashion of doing one's own thing with the themes of another poet. I have designated *Nightmares* as one of the most Rilkean of contemporary American long poems; that appraisal is intended as a verification of Kinnell as a postmodernist, since Rilke is the early twentieth-century poet who has special affinities with the postmodernist sensibility of the post-1960s. It may be extravagant to compare Galway Kinnell with the great poets he admired—Whitman, Yeats, Frost—or with the great poets he has translated so well, Villon and Rilke. But he should be judged with his postmodernist contemporaries and peers, James Wright, Richard Hugo, Gary Snyder, and James Dickey, all of whom in their diverse ways have been in their poetry set against technology as well.

If Galway Kinnell can be faulted for being "unrelenting" and seeking to see everything as a "crucial event," he should be credited with the ultimate concern of the existential fifties so permanently influential on some of the writers of his generation. His concern with death, with the mutability of all living things, with his large apocalyptic image, as David Perkins has characterized it, of "darkness enveloping a frozen earth," might turn some readers off as too unrelentingly bleak (Perkins, 575). Yet he has longed for more life, not extinction. To alleviate some of the gloom, he has even had his taste for little ironies, a knack for self-mockery, a sense of humor even if it does sometimes come close to gallows humor. To David Perkins's statement that "God was absent from his cosmos but not from his emotions for he longed to merge with the transcendent" (Perkins, 575), I would add a further qualification, all this written while doubting the possibility of transcendence.

I would close with stress on what may be relevant for Kinnell's poetry in the 1990s. An important change may have taken place in his poetry, beginning in the 1970s. He has attempted to turn from his sometimes seemingly portentous earlier subjects to realize some of the same meaning from more ordinary experiences. Lee Zimmerman finds in Kinnell's 1985 *The Past* a concern with the danger of losing "all touch with humanity," but he also acknowledges that the poet is engaged in "the search for right relation" (Zimmerman, 231). Among his most effective and most affirmative poems searching for this "right relation" are those that put to use what has also grown in his poetry into a saga of his two children, Fergus and Maud. Kinnell's most convincing poems emotionally may be those in which he declares in middle-age a father's devoted love for wife and children.

Charles Molesworth and other critics have detected a movement away from the distanced irony in treatment of some of his subjects, an attitude more characteristic of modernist writers, towards the empathy and involvement favored among most postmodernist poets. Galway Kinnell has clearly exhibited sufficient empathy to deserve comparison and contrast, perhaps not with the master Whitman, but with James Dickey, who is known for his own empathetic "way of exchange."[1] Kinnell is assuredly not in any way an imitation of Dickey. He can be as powerful as Dickey even though he is less melodramatic in narrative and less immodest as persona. Kinnell did not surge quickly to the top in poetic reputation as Dickey did with his first notice in the 1960s, but he has risen steadily in critical reputation as Dickey has declined precipitously.

Galway Kinnell also deserves credit as a poet whose empathy has led him into the political realm, into personal engagement in political activities against segregation and against nuclear weapons and even into the writing of some of the better political poetry since the 1960s. There is a current interest in political poetry and political poets, and Kinnell's poems in this vein deserve attention. He is one of the surprisingly few American writers who—like Thoreau—have been jailed for taking a stand against unjust local laws.

In an essay for the *Iowa Review,* reprinted in Stephen Berg and Robert Mezey's *The New Naked Poetry,* Galway Kinnell has defined the kind of poetry he has intended as a poetics of the physical world. He has distinguished this poetry from another kind he has chosen not to write, the poetics of Heaven. "The poetics of Heaven agrees to the denigration of pain and death; the poetics of the physical world builds on these stones" (*PPW,* 119). The poetry he has built on these "stones" intensified in the seventies until it encompassed an empathetic immersion in nature. There are dangers in this kind of immersion, in too much empathy, and Kinnell acknowledges them; however, he has tried to make clear in his own commentary what has not always been clearly perceived by his critics. His empathy is not just with extinction but also with the neoromantic desire for more life. He explains: "We may note that the desire to be some other thing is itself suicidal; it involves a willingness to cease to be a man. But this is not a simple wish for extinction so much as it is a desire for union with what is loved. And so it is a desire for more, not less, life" (*PPW,* 124).

What exactly does Kinnell want to tell in his poetry about final things, about extinction? He may say it best in what has already been quoted from his essay "Poetry, Personality, and Death." His concern with death is with a hope of being reborn, "more alive, more open, more related to natural life" (*PPD,* 222). Kinnell has been acknowledged as a neoromantic, but he is clearly also an empiricist in that knowledge for him comes from what one perceives in nature through the senses. He is a poet who worries about a dissociation of sensibility or Cartesian split between the claims of reason and the claims of intuition. His own poetry has attempted to explore the mystery that Roethke defined for the lyric poet: "He works intuitively, and the final form of his poem must be imaginatively right."[2] Galway Kinnell has been "imaginatively right" in enough poems to be acknowledged as one of our major poets writing today.

Kinnell has always emphasized not just death but the process of life and death, a life in which death must be recognized as having a part. His entry with poetic empathy into the lives of his two children changed the sense of isolation and of emptiness in the nightmare visions characteristic of his earlier poems. By the end of *The Book of Nightmares* and extending over into his next book, *The Past,* Kinnell has come to see that poetry, like the music of a Bach concert, can be the resolution of all individually felt pain.

How many major poems has Kinnell written? Or as Randall Jarrell used to say about poetic genius: how many times has the lightning struck? It is a matter of judgment, and judgments will differ. But I can offer my own favorites, reinforced by the usual anthology selections, poems in my judgment to know the poet by. My own choices would include: "Freedom, New Hampshire," "The Avenue Bearing the Initial of Christ into the New World," "For Robert Frost," "Flower Herding on Mount Monadnock," "Vapor Trail Reflected in the Frog Pond," "The

Porcupine," "The Bear," "Under Maud Moon," "Fergus Falling," "Wait," "Flying Home," "Little Sleep's-Head Sprouting Hair in the Moonlight," "Saint Francis and the Sow," and "The Fundamental Project of Technology."

One really cannot stop there, by naming only the poems. Galway Kinnell is a man of letters, poet, novelist, serious commentator on poetry, and a major translator. His interviews and occasional essays are informative comments on his own poetry and rare judgments on the poetry of others. He is a good interviewee, and editor of his own interviews on his poetry. He is a significant translator. It is beyond the province of this survey to comment on his translations; but it has been noted that his *Poems of François Villon* is one of the finer translations by a contemporary American poet of a significant French poet. Here again, Kinnell is better at the long poems. His translation of Villon's "The Testament" compares with the translations of longer works, mostly dramatic, by Richard Wilbur. As poet, critic, novelist, and translator, Galway Kinnell is clearly one of our important men of letters.

Finally, if Kinnell is his own version of a postmodernist, he also has one of the best claims among his contemporaries of maintaining the Whitman tradition—again his own distinctive version. His early essay, "Whitman's Indicative Words," was reprinted in a collection of scholarly essays on Whitman and in a definitive edition of his work. His interest in Whitman persists. In 1987 Kinnell became editor as well as critic and fellow poet by editing his own selection in *The Essential Whitman*.[3] In 1989 on the Whitman film for the "Voices and Visions" television series, he proved a better commentator on Whitman's poetry than another fractious disciple, Allen Ginsberg. Whitman's mistake as a poet, as Kinnell sees it, was that he forgot as his fame grew that his great poem was not about himself, Walter Whitman, but about "a representative man, a workman-poet," as Whitman himself described his persona, "Walt Whitman, an American, one of the roughs, a kosmos." The new persona took on a more conventional style. In the ways I have indicated, Kinnell has become more personal; but he endeavors not to lose the representational aspect of his early poems. He has always sought and continues to seek a balance between his urge to express the emotions of his private self and the necessity of taking a stance, even in poetry, on public issues. Above all, still central is his human need to identify with all the living creatures of the natural world, to understand the morality required of a conscious living creature facing the mortality of all creatures. He has found the exact style capable of expressing all these concerns. He may adjust it but he has not changed it radically.

Why does Galway Kinnell continue to write poetry in a time of 10-second sound-bytes on television? He has recently eloquently confirmed that he will continue to write for the sheer pleasure of the experience of reaching a higher level of consciousness than the merely private.

Some kind of inner release takes place where you fall into a deeper concentration and all of your inhibitions and self-consciousness disappear and that surface level of you becomes just a medium, just a scribe racing to write down what something in a lower, deeper level of consciousness is producing. And so I would hope that at that deeper level of consciousness there is not only the man or the woman who any given writer is but there's also the man and the woman that every person is. (*BWR,* 178)

Notes and References

Chapter One

1. Charles G. Bell, "Galway Kinnell," in *On the Poetry of Galway Kinnell*, ed. by Howard Nelson (Ann Arbor: University of Michigan Press, 1986), 25; hereafter cited in text.

2. Emory Elliott, ed., *Columbia Literary History of the United States* (New York: Columbia University Press, 1988), 1094–96.

3. James Dickey, *Babel to Byzantium: Poets and Poetry Now* (New York: Farrar, Straus and Giroux, 1968), 135; hereafter cited in text.

4. Donald Hall, 'Text as Test," in Howard Nelson, 163.

Chapter Two

1. Monroe K. Spears, *Dionysus and the City: Modernism in Twentieth-Century Poetry* (London, New York: Oxford University Press, 1970).

2. David Perkins, *A History of Modern Poetry: Modernism and After* (Cambridge, Mass. and London, 1987), 339; hereafter cited in text.

3. Charles Molesworth, *The Fierce Embrace* (Columbia, Mo.: University of Missouri Press, 1979), 100; hereafter cited in text.

4. Benjamin De Mott, "The 'More Life' School and James Dickey," *Saturday Review,* 28 March 1970, 38.

Chapter Three

1. *Walking Down the Stairs* (Ann Arbor: University of Michigan Press, 1978). This collection includes all the major interviews from 1969 to 1976.

2. Randall Jarrell, *Poetry and the Age* (New York: Ecco Press, 1953).

3. James Dickey, *Self-Interviews,* recorded and edited by Barbara and James Reiss (Garden City, New York: Doubleday & Company, 1970).

4. Lee Zimmerman, *Intricate and Simple Things: The Poetry of Galway Kinnell* (Urbana and Chicago: The University of Illinois Press, 1987), 195; hereafter cited in text.

5. "Poetry, Personality and Death," in *A Field Guide to Contemporary Poetry and Poetics,* ed. by Stuart Friebert and Donald Young (New York: Longman, 1980), 203–23. Originally appeared in *Field,* no. 4 (Spring 1971): 56–75.

Chapter Four

1. The first publication was *First Poems 1946–1954* (Mt. Horeb, Wis.: Perishable Press, 1970). These early poems were later published in the much more

accessible volume *The Avenue Bearing the Initial of Christ into the New World: Poems 1946–1964* (Boston: Houghton Mifflin, 1974). My references are to the later book, which is the edition that I have used.

2. Ralph J. Mills, *Cry of the Human* (Urbana: University of Illinois Press, 1975), 143; hereafter cited in text.

3. Louise Bogan, "Verse," *New Yorker,* 1 April 1961, 130. Reprinted in Howard Nelson.

4. Cleanth Brooks, *Modern Poetry and the Tradition* (Chapel Hill: University of North Carolina Press, 1939).

5. Donald Davie, "Slogging for the Absolute," in Howard Nelson, 143–56; hereafter cited in text.

6. Kenneth F. Weaver and Jonathan Blair, "Meteorites: Invaders from Space," *National Geographic* 170 (Sept. 1986): 391–418.

7. Christopher Ricks, "In the Direct Line of Whitman, the Indirect Line of Eliot," in Howard Nelson, 93–94.

8. Seldon Rodman, "A Quartet of Younger Singers," *New York Times Book Review,* 18 September 1960, 50.

9. John Logan, "Fine First Book," *Commonweal,* 4 November 1960, 154–56.

10. Glauco Cambon, *Recent American Poetry* (Minneapolis: University of Minnesota Press, 1961), 31.

11. Cary Nelson, "Ecclesiastical Whitman: on 'The Avenue Bearing the Initial of Christ into the World,'" in Howard Nelson, 187; hereafter cited in text.

12. Paul Mariani, "Kinnell's Legacy: on 'The Avenue Bearing the Initial of Christ into the New World,'" in Howard Nelson, 191; hereafter cited in text.

Chapter Five

1. Yves Bonnefoy, *On the Motion and Immobility of Douve,* trans. Galway Kinnell (Athens: Ohio University Press, 1968).

2. Geoffrey Thurley, *The American Moment: American Poetry in the Mid-Century* (London: Edward Arnold Publisher, 1977), 213.

Chapter Six

1. Andrew Taylor, "The Poetry of Galway Kinnell," in Howard Nelson, 40.

Chapter Seven

1. Norman O. Brown, *Life Against Death* (Middletown, Conn.: Wesleyan University Press, 1957), 138; hereafter cited in text.

2. M. L. Rosenthal, "Under the Freeway, in the Hotel of Lost Light," in Howard Nelson, 85.

3. "The Weight a Poem Can Carry," interviewed by Wayne Dodd and Stanley Plumly, the *Ohio Review,* no. 14 (Fall 1972): 35. The version in *Walking Down the Stairs* has been slightly edited by Kinnell.

Chapter Eight

1. Harold Bloom, "Straight Forth Out of Self," *New York Times Book Review,* 22 June 1980, 13; hereafter cited in the text.

2. Hank Lazer, "That Backward-Spreading Brightness," in Howard Nelson, 108; hereafter cited in text.

3. John Unterecker, "Of Father, of Son: On 'Fergus Falling,' 'After Making Love We Hear Footsteps,' and 'Angling, A Day,'" in Howard Nelson, 227; hereafter cited in text.

Chapter Nine

1. *The Essential Whitman,* selected with an Introduction by Galway Kinnell (New York: The Ecco Press, 1987), 210; hereafter referred to in text as *EW.*

2. "New Poems by Beloit Poets of the 50s," *Beloit Poetry Journal* 40, no. 4 (Summer 1990): 36–37.

3. "The Perch," *New Yorker,* 10 September 1990, 42.

4. "The Judas-Kiss," *New Yorker,* 15 October 1990, 50.

5. *Poems of François Villon* (New York: New American Library, 1965; rev. ed., Boston: Houghton Mifflin, 1977).

Chapter Ten

1. See H. L. Weatherby, "The Way of Exchange in James Dickey's Poetry," in *James Dickey: The Expansive Imagination,* ed. Richard J. Calhoun (Deland, Fla: Everett / Edwards, Inc. pp. 53–64.

2. "Open Letter," in *On the Poet and His Craft: Selected Prose of Theodore Roethke,* ed. Ralph J. Mills (Seattle: University of Washington Press, 1965), 42.

3. *Walt Whitman: The Measure of His Song,* ed. Jim Perlman, Ed Folsom, and Dan Campion (Minneapolis: Holy Cow! Press, 1981) 215–227. Bibliographical reference for *EW* is footnote 1, chapter 9.

Selected Bibliography

PRIMARY WORKS

Poetry

The Avenue Bearing the Initial of Christ into the New World: Poems 1946–1964. Boston: Houghton Mifflin, 1974.

Body Rags. Boston: Houghton Mifflin, 1968.

The Book of Nightmares. Boston: Houghton Mifflin, 1971.

First Poems 1946–1954. Mt. Horeb, Wis.: Perishable Press, 1970.

Flower Herding on Mount Monadnock. Boston: Houghton Mifflin, 1964.

Mortal Acts, Mortal Words. Boston: Houghton Mifflin, 1980.

The Past. Boston: Houghton Mifflin, 1985.

Selected Poems. Boston: Houghton Mifflin, 1982.

The Shoes of Wandering. Mt. Horeb, Wis.: Perishable Press, 1971.

Three Poems. New York: Phoenix Book Shop, 1976.

What a Kingdom It Was. Boston: Houghton Mifflin, 1960.

When One Has Lived a Long Time Alone. New York: Alfred A. Knopf, 1990.

Translations

Bitter Victory, by Rene Hardy. New York: Doubleday, 1956. Novel.

Lackawanna Elegy, by Yvan Goll. Fremont, Mich.: Sumac, 1970. Poems.

On the Motion and Immobility of Douve, by Yves Bonnefoy. Athens, Ohio: Ohio University Press, 1968. Poems.

The Poems of François Villon. New York: New American Library, 1965. Rev. ed. Boston: Houghton Mifflin, 1977. Poems.

Fiction

Black Light. Boston: Houghton Mifflin, 1966. Rev. ed. San Francisco: North Point Press, 1981. Novel.

How the Alligator Missed Breakfast. Boston: Houghton Mifflin, 1982. Children's book.

Nonfiction

Foreword to *The Selected Poetry of Hayden Carruth.* New York: Collier/Macmillan, 1985.

"Last of the Big-Time Amateurs." *Sports Illustrated,* 25 June 1973, 30–32, 37–40.

Note on "The Supper After the Last." In *Poet's Choice.* Edited by Paul Engle and Joseph Langland, 257. New York: Delta, 1966.

"Only Meaning is Truly Interesting." *Beloit Poetry Journal* 4 (Fall 1953): 1–3.

"Poetry, Personality, and Death." *Field,* no. 4 (Spring 1971): 56–75. Reprinted in *A Field Guide to Contemporary Poetry and Poetics,* edited by Stuart Friebert and David Young, 203–23. New York: Longman, 1980.

"Poets Against the End of the World." *Poetry East,* no. 9/10 (Winter 1982/Spring 1983): 16–23. Introduction with interview.

"The Poetics of the Physical World." *Iowa Review* 2 (Summer 1971): 113–26. Reprinted in part in *The New Naked Poetry,* edited by Stephen Berg and Robert Mezey. Indianapolis: Bobbs-Merrill, 1976.

Postscript to *Eternity's Woods* by Paul Zweig. Middletown, Conn.: Wesleyan University Press, 1985.

Review of *Songs for a New America,* by Charles G. Bell. *Beloit Poetry Journal* 5 (Summer 1955): 29–32.

"Whitman's Indicative Words." *American Poetry Review* 2 (March/April 1973): 9–11. Revised version in *Walt Whitman: The Measure of His Song,* edited by Jim Perlman, Ed Folsom, and Dan Campion, 215–27. Minneapolis: Holy Cow! Press, 1981.

Interviews

"Being with Reality: An Interview with Galway Kinnell." *Columbia: A Magazine of Poetry and Prose,* no. 14 (1989): 169–82.

Walking Down the Stairs: Selections from Interviews. Ann Arbor: University of Michigan Press, 1978. The collected and somewhat edited interviews dated back through 1968. Since these are interviews as Kinnell wanted them to appear, I have not listed the original printings.

Illustrations

The Snow Rabbit, by Pati Hill. Boston: Houghton Mifflin, 1962. Poems.

Recordings

Galway Kinnell: Interviews and Readings. Brockport, N. Y.: Brockport Writers Forum, State University of New York, 1972. Videotape.

Galway Kinnell. San Francisco: American Poetry Archive and Resource Center, San Francisco State University, 1975. Videotape.

The Poetry of Galway Kinnell. New York: Jeffrey Norton Publishers/McGraw Hill, 1965. Audiocassette.

SECONDARY SOURCES

Critical Studies

Altieri, Charles. *Self and Sensibility in Contemporary American Poetry.* New York: Cambridge University Press, 1984. Altieri argues that in his *Book of Nightmares* Galway Kinnell is not able "to elaborate a metaphysical scheme equal to his demonic moments and capacious enough to justify a fully bardic stance." There are "often brilliant nightmare visions" but "Kinnell's ideas are very thin" and he is "forced to rely on the verbal gestures of intense emotion grafted onto conventional romantic postures."

Bell, Charles G. "Galway Kinnell." In *Contemporary Poets,* 3d ed., edited by James Vinson, 835–37. New York: St. Martin's Press, 1980. Overall view of Kinnell as a major poet written by his former teacher and longtime friend.

Bellamy, Joe David, ed. *American Poetry Observed: Poets on Their Work.* Urbana: University of Illinois Press, 1984. An interview with Kinnell made in 1978 mainly on his most recent book then, *The Book of Nightmares.* Bellamy comments on Kinnell's occasional use of archaic language, on his family ("one writes not about spectacular events but about the normal events"), and on his translations.

Berke, Robert A. *Bounds Out of Bounds.* New York: Oxford University Press, 1981. Kinnell's poetry undertakes a wide scope of subjects made real by vivid imagery and "tense pared-down lines." At his best he shows the human caught with other creatures in huge issues of life and death.

Bly, Robert. "Galway Kinnell and the Old Farmer." In Howard Nelson, 178–84. Bly discusses two movements in Kinnell's poetry. One is "down into earthly body, dirt, appetite, gross desire, death." The other contrasting movement is "toward sunlight, time, fulfillment, lily blossoms, purity, narcissus flowers, beauty, opening." There are two separate beings in conversation in his poetry, one of moments of transfiguration. Another being, ancient and powerful, "remains in matter," identified in the poem "Farm Picture" in *The Past* as the old farmer, who lives by being attached.

Bruchac, Joseph. "I Have Come to Myself Empty: Galway Kinnell's Bear and Porcupine." In Howard Nelson, 203–9. A comparison of Kinnell's two most noted animal poems, showing how Kinnell begins with the physical body of animals and with death and transcends them through use of Rilke and the religions and people of the Near East. He is expert in his knowledge of the physical animals and their symbolic and mythical meanings.

Cambon, Glauco. *Recent American Poetry*. Minneapolis: University of Minnesota Press, 1962. Early mention of Kinnell's poetry in a brief standard survey of contemporary poetry.

———. "Dante on Galway Kinnell's 'Last River.'" In *Dante's Influence on American Writers 1776–1976*, edited by Anne Paolucci, 31–39. New York: Griffon House, 1976. A convincing demonstration of an influence not stressed by other critics.

Comito, Terry. "Slogging Toward the Absolute." *Modern Poetry Studies* 6 (1975): 189–92. In "slogging toward the absolute" Kinnell pays tribute to "the dense and stubborn particularity of the world." His colloquial tone also associates him with Dickinson and Frost who faced the temptations of the night, as Kinnell does, but retained a commitment to working consciousness.

Davie, Donald. "Slogging for the Absolute." *Parnassus* 3 (Fall/Winter 1974): 9–22. Reprinted in his *The Poet in the Imaginary Museum*. New York: Persea Books, 1979. Also in Howard Nelson, 143–56. Davie is both an admirer of Kinnell's potential and a worrier about his lack of serious theological or Christian content. This apparent disdain is the negative factor on which Davie would lecture Kinnell.

Dickey, James. *Babel to Byzantium: Poets and Poetry Now*. New York: Farrar, Straus and Giroux, 1968. An important early recognition of Kinnell's poetic potential by a poet with whom Kinnell has been often compared.

Gallagher, Tess. "The Poem as a Reservoir for Grief." *American Poetry Review* 13 (July/August 1984): 7–11. Reprinted in her *A Concert of Tenses*. Ann Arbor: University of Michigan Press, 1986. A brief examination of the negative in Kinnell's poetry in relation to the structure of the poems.

Guimond, James. *Seeing and Healing: A Study of the Poetry of Galway Kinnell*. Port Washington, N. Y.: Associated Faculty Press, 1984. The first book on Kinnell, a good introductory survey of the major themes of Kinnell's poetry.

Hall, Donald. 'Text as Test: Notes on and around Carruth and Kinnell." *American Poetry Review* 12 (November/December 1983): 27–32.

Hilberry, Conrad. "The Structure of Galway Kinnell's *The Book of Nightmares*." *Field*, no. 12 (Spring 1975): 28–46. A detailed analysis of this book of poetry. Still one of the most convincing accounts of the structure.

Hoffman, Daniel, ed. *Harvard Guide to Contemporary American Writing*. Cambridge, Mass.: Harvard University Press. Belknap Press, 1979, 566–70. A good overall account of Kinnell's work up to the late 1970s tracing his early interest in Yeats. There is special concern with Kinnell's fire imagery and his relationship in his poems with both living and dead creatures. A new tenderness is noted with the entrance of his children into his poetry. Hoffman finds a positive "resurgent life-force" in his poetry capable of transcending the nightmares.

Howard, Richard, "Galway Kinnell." In *Alone with America: Essays on the Art of Poetry in America since 1950.* New York: Atheneum, 1969, 304–19. The focus is on Kinnell's poetry as "an Ordeal by Fire," on the fire imagery. It is fire that is reality for Kinnell as it was for Heraclitus. The passion of his poetry is in the knowledge that he is part of "the world's physics," of the same force with which the earth burns. Included is a brief review of Kinnell's fourth book, *The Book of Nightmares.*

Hudgins, Andrew. "One and Zero Walk Off Together: Dualism in Galway Kinnell's *The Book of Nightmares.*" *American Poetry* 3 (Fall 1985): 56–71.

Malkoff, Karl. *Crowell's Handbook of Contemporary American Poetry.* New York: Thomas Y. Crowell, 1973. This is a good standard survey of Kinnell's work up until the early 1970s.

Mariani, Paul. "Kinnell's Legacy: On 'The Avenue Bearing the Initial of Christ into the New World.'" In Howard Nelson, 191–203. Mariani views this major poem as a young man's poem, "brash, sardonic, hardbitten, overreaching, vulnerable, earnest, vital," and reveals this richness of the poem through all its implicit references. Mariani is especially good on the relationship of this poem to Whitman and Hart Crane.

Marusilak, Joe. "Where We Might Meet Each Other: An Appreciation of Galway Kinnell and William Everson." *Literary Review* 24 (Spring 1981): 355–70. A comparison and contrast of themes and subjects. Each poet in his different way is an important contemporary poet.

Matthews, William. "On the Tennis Court at Night." In Howard Nelson, 242–50. A statement of Kinnell's serious interest in the game of tennis. Matthews argues that in the dual power Kinnell finds in tennis, body and spirit emerge; at the same time, one gains more life and becomes more like a wild animal. This is the power his poetry celebrates. (Analyzes in detail "On the Tennis Court at Night.")

Medwick, Cathleen. "Poetry in Motion." *Vogue* 185 (November 1985): 280–81. Kinnell's poetic voice attempts to remind us over the noises of our civilization that there is music which rules the lives of other creatures more than it does ours. We can hear this music directly in nature through the singing of insects or through music and poetry.

Mills, Ralph J. "A Reading of Galway Kinnell." In his *Cry of the Human.* Urbana: University of Illinois Press, 1975, 134–91. This is a major analysis of Kinnell's poetry in his first three books, *What a Kingdom It Was, Flower Herding on Mount Monadnock,* and *Body Rags.* It is still one of the best discussions of themes, structure, and imagery of major poems in the first three books, providing the reader with a sense of immediacy and with the flow of his own thoughts. The growth of his poetry is in close congruence with his life as James Dickey early predicted it must be. Both poets have learned from Lawrence that "much of poetry comes from below the head."

Molesworth, Charles. "'The Rank Flavor of Blood': The Poetry of Galway Kinnell." In *The Fierce Embrace.* Columbia, Mo.: University of Missouri Press, 1979, 98–112. Kinnell's poetry's demonstrates how the poet can do some justice to the complexity of experience by turning to his own divided consciousness as his chief subject. Kinnell is one of those poets who present the consciousness directly while "qualifying the mind that observes it." His special trait is the ability to rediscover how to view objects intensely, "while continuing to avoid any prescribed system." He is concerned powerfully with both "self-discovery and self-destruction."

Nelson, Cary. "Ecclesiastical Whitman: On 'The Avenue Bearing the Initial of Christ into the New World.'" In Howard Nelson, 187–190. A selection from a longer essay on *The Book of Nightmares* printed in Cary Nelson's book noted in following listing.

———. *Our Last First Poets: Vision and History in Contemporary American Poetry.* Urbana: University of Illinois Press, Illini Books, 1984. The most informative close reading of *The Book of Nightmares.*

Nelson, Howard, ed. *On the Poetry of Galway Kinnell.* Ann Arbor: University of Michigan Press, 1987. This is the best collection of previously published material on Kinnell with a few new essays. The most useful essays are listed in this bibliography.

———. "The Weight of Words, the Road from Here to There." In Howard Nelson, 1–19. This is a discussion of the positive ways in which Kinnell's poetic language is weighty. The imagery is an obvious reason for this impression created by his poetry. He must also characteristically find the spiritual in earthly things. He also has a great love of words, illustrated by his poem "Blackberries." His poetic recognition of "emptiness" comes from "an insight into the nature of things." Kinnell belongs in an important modern tradition—which includes Yeats, Frost, Stevens—that tries to move from this negative to revelation.

Parris, Peggy. "Rags of His Body: Thoreau in Galway Kinnell's 'The Last River.'" *Thoreau Society Bulletin* 161 (Fall 1982): 4–6. Parris does a comparison-contrast analysis based on the Thoreau reference in this political poem.

Peters, Robert. *The Great American Poetry Bake-off.* Metuchen, N. J.: Scarecrow Press, 1979.

Rich, Adrienne. "Poetry, Personality and Wholeness." *Field,* no. 7 (Fall 1972): 11–18. Reprinted in *A Field Guide to Contemporary Poetry,* edited by Stuart Friebert and David Young, 224–32. New York: Longman, 1980. Kinnell's problem as a poet is seen as that of the masculine writer, how to break free of the masculine language and "handed-down myths" and to face "his fear and guilt towards women."

Rosenthal, M. L., and Sally M. Gall. *The Modern Poetic Sequence.* New York: Oxford University Press, 1983. The text is mostly concerned with *The Book of Nightmares.* It finds the image of war powerful in his poetry and also concludes that Kinnell does not "permit the drastically negative to prevail in any one poem."

Solotaroff, Ted. "Knowing and Not Knowing." In *Singular Voices,* edited by Stephen Berg, 137–42. New York: Avon, 1985.

Taylor, Andrew. "The Poetry of Galway Kinnell." *Meanjin* 36 (July 1977): 228–39.

Thurley, Geoffrey. *The American Moment.* New York: St. Martin's Press, 1977, 211–218. A discussion of "The Avenue Bearing the Initial of Christ in to the New World" that finds the Jewish references offensive, and with no effective sense of a poetic voice. Kinnell is at his best when his subtle Platonism has its roots in rural experience.

Unterecker, John. "Of Father, of Son: On 'Fergus Falling,' 'After Making Love We Hear Footsteps,' and 'Angling, a Day.'" In Howard Nelson, 227–42. Unterecker argues for the three Fergus poems as essential to the structure and themes of *Mortal Acts, Mortal Words.* They are opening notes in establishing the musical context of the structure of the poems in the book.

Wagner, Linda. "'Spindrift': The World in a Seashell." *Concerning Poetry* 8 (Spring 1975): 5–9.

Weston, Susan B. "Galway Kinnell's *Walking Down the Stairs.*" *Iowa Review* 10, no. 1 (1970): 95–98.

White, Marshal Peterson. "Trusting the Hours: on 'Wait.'" In Howard Nelson, 251–66. White regards this short poem as both a typical Kinnell poem and one of his masterpieces, echoing both Eliot and Roethke. The theme, one of Kinnell's central themes, is "that love and loss are inextricably bound together."

Williamson, Alan. *Introspection and Contemporary Poetry.* Cambridge, Mass: Harvard University Press, 1984. Williamson attempts to broaden the meaning of "confessional poetry" by seeing this mode as a means, for poets like Kinnell, to gain first self-absorption and then a perspective for the examination of the self.

Wright, Anne. "Sitting on Top of the Sunlight." In Howard Nelson, 275–84. James Wright's wife's account of a visit by the Kinnells after he had finished his teaching stint at Reed College and the continuing friendship of the two poets until Wright's death from cancer.

Young, David. "Galway Kinnell." In *The Longman Anthology of Contemporary American Poetry 1950–80,* edited by David Young and Stuart Friebert, 241–44. New York: Longman, 1983. Recent survey of Kinnell's work up until the 1980s.

Zimmerman, Lee. *Intricate and Simple Things: The Poetry of Galway Kinnell.* Urbana and Chicago: University of Illinois Press, 1987. The most comprehensive study of Kinnell's poetry so far. Zimmerman contends that Kinnell's poetry dramatizes two different feelings—strangeness and terrible kinship—about the relationship between ourselves and "what is beyond us." This philosophical dualism results structurally in his poems in "an unreconciled conflict between pairs."

Index

The Author

Richard James Calhoun received his Ph.D. in American literature from the University of North Carolina in Chapel Hill in 1959. He has taught at Davidson College in North Carolina from 1958–61 and at Clemson University in South Carolina since 1961, where he has been Alumni Professor of English since 1968. He has written with Robert Hill the Twayne volume on James Dickey and edited a study of Dickey's poetry, *James Dickey: The Expansive Imagination.* With John C. Guilds, Jr., he edited *The Tricentennial Anthology of South Carolina Literature.* His most recent work is *Witness to Sorrow: The Antebellum Autobiography of William J. Grayson.* Since 1986 he has edited the chapter "Poetry since 1940" for *American Literary Scholarship.*

He has been president of the Society for the Study of Southern Literature and of the Robert Frost Society. During 1969–70 he was Fulbright lecturer at the University of Ljubljana and the University of Sarajevo in Yugoslavia and during 1975–76 at Aarhus University and Odense University in Denmark. He resides with his wife Doris, in Clemson, South Carolina, where he edits the *South Carolina Review.*

The Editor

Frank Day is a professor of English at Clemson University. He is the author of *Sir William Empson: An Annotated Bibliography* and *Arthur Koestler: A Guide to Research.* He was a Fulbright Lecturer in American Literature in Romania (1980–81) and in Bangladesh (1986–87).